BASICS

PRODUC[T]

03

David Bramston

visual conversations

Ethical: awareness/ reflection/ debate

ava academia

An AVA Book

Published by AVA Publishing SA
Rue des Fontenailles 16
Case Postale
1000 Lausanne 6
Switzerland
Tel: +41 786 005 109
Email: enquiries@avabooks.ch

Distributed by Thames & Hudson (ex-North America)
181a High Holborn
London WC1V 7QX
United Kingdom
Tel: +44 20 7845 5000
Fax: +44 20 7845 5055
Email: sales@thameshudson.co.uk
www.thamesandhudson.com

Distributed in the USA and Canada by:
Ingram Publisher Services Inc.
1 Ingram Blvd.
La Vergne TN 37086
USA
Tel: +1 866 400 5351
Fax: +1 800 838 1149
Email: customer.service@ingrampublisherservices.com

English Language Support Office
AVA Publishing (UK) Ltd.
Tel: +44 1903 204 455
Email: enquiries@avabooks.ch

ISBN 978-2-940411-09-2
10 9 8 7 6 5 4 3 2 1

Design by Malcolm Southward

Production by AVA Book Production Pte. Ltd, Singapore
Tel: +65 6334 8173
Fax: +65 6259 9830
Email: production@avabooks.com.sg

All reasonable attempts have been made
to trace, clear and credit the copyright holders
of the images reproduced in this book.
However, if any credits have been inadvertently
omitted, the publisher will endeavour to
incorporate amendments in future editions.

Right: Accidental Carpet, Tejo Remy and
René Veenhuizen.

Cover image: 'Bocca' stool, Barnaba Fornasetti, 2005.

Contents

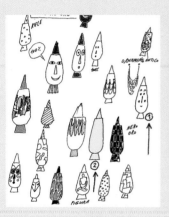  

Visual conversations

Contents

Basics Product Design: Visual Conversations explores the communication and narrative of ideas along with the subsequent processes that can be followed to retain and effectively communicate the story within an inanimate object. The inherent story, hidden messages and the shrouded themes of products are also considered, along with the development and make-up of the product.

A conversation is usually a communication of messages between individuals that gives those involved an opportunity to exchange thoughts and opinions, reflect on experiences and, where necessary, seek affirmation. A conversation can be a temporary or momentary connection, a fleeting process that summarises a feeling, but it can also be a captivating encounter that is engaging and challenging for both parties.

The impressions and perceptions that are constantly conjured up by creative dialogue are continually deciphered, assimilated and consumed by listeners and observers in order to establish a connection between what is being said and their own experiences and associations. When a story is conveyed in a literary sense, it relies on the receiver attempting to accurately fill in the gaps and ascertain or find appropriate meanings. The recipient needs to absorb all possible sensory indicators and attempt to make the necessary mental connections in order to substantiate and accept the meaning and context. The communication does not need to be protracted or complex for a listener to grasp the fundamental aspects of a conversation, providing that it is appropriately delivered and considered. If a story is communicated in a manner whereby opportunities to interpret and anticipate influential elements are not presented, the process can become sterile, dull and somewhat repressed. Dictatorial expression does not readily entertain and is often restrictive and unappealing to an audience due to its limited creativity.

The intriguing, random and nomadic nature of imagination responds to descriptive triggers, and an abstract language often stimulates a continuous sequence of thoughts and unique impressions. The imagination needs freedom to translate and interpret information as it arrives. Although the impression may not be identical to that which the storyteller was trying to project, basic modification and reconfiguration by the receiver allows it to be consumed and digested in a fashion that is appropriate to them.

Although most people think of conversations as being purely verbal, they are often assisted by visual characteristics and expressions. These characteristics are often required to project valuable and meaningful messages to a variety of different audiences. For example, a storyteller is able to enhance a tale by using different facial expressions to convey the mood of the characters he describes. The environment that the story is told in also helps to communicate with the audience – a ghost story told in a dark, creaky old house is more effective than

Self-reflecting lamp
The self-reflecting lamp is a black 'desktop lamp' designed by Oliver Schick and part of the designer's experimental works collection that considers the function of objects.

Design
Oliver Schick

Photography
Michael Himpel

Chapter 1
Speaking visually

The various ways that ideas are initially identified and communicated using different approaches are introduced along with the relevance of mnemonic indicators. Chapter 1 also explores the significance of a simple and effective suggestion that can deliver a clear visual message. The methods and techniques used by other, non-product design disciplines are also explored and considered.

Chapter 2
Emotional responses

Chapter 2 explores the methods of communicating the feeling and soul of an idea through the creative use of 2D and 3D mixed media and different emotional approaches. The relevance of size and texture within a communication strategy, along with different approaches to such work, is also examined.

Chapter 3
Seeing the gap

Appreciating what others are communicating and how to interpret such messages forms the basis of Chapter 3. Noticing the hidden detail and understanding what is actually being communicated through gesture, implied meanings, facial expressions or a statement is crucial to this chapter.

Chapter 4
Talking aesthetically

The aesthetic language of a product is a powerful and emotive tool, which is capable of both suggestion and deceit. In Chapter 4, the use of aesthetics to portray different and mixed messages is investigated using a broad array of examples. The importance of surface treatment, the skin and the finish of a product are explored using historical and contemporary examples.

Chapter 5
Taming the thought

Selecting examples from a broad range of design offices, Chapter 5 looks at how information can be communicated with character and fun, avoiding potential problems and visual constraints. The language and being of the product is considered along with how an animated life changes perceptions of products.

Chapter 6
Performing

The art of communication can be conducted using a broad range of methods to ensure the correct message is presented properly. The actual presentation is similar to taking the stage; it is a performance that needs to be rehearsed and practised to ensure that the essential issues are delivered coherently and appropriately. Chapter 6 looks at the different ways that a presentation can be conducted and examines some common mistakes.

get the most out of this book

How to get the most out of this book

Visual Conversations aims to encourage an appreciation of the various sensory narratives within design and help design students to develop an awareness of how a product can be composed to communicate different messages. Using a broad range of examples, the book focuses on the aesthetic function of ideas and demonstrates how subtle differences can radically influence interaction and emotional dialogues. In addition, *Visual Conversations* identifies useful processes and aims to stimulate creative design thinking.

Quotations
Help to place the topic being discussed into context by conveying the views and thoughts of designers and artists.

'A sketch is generally more spirited than a picture.'
Denis Diderot, philosopher, art critic and writer

Keeping it simple

A simple design is often anything but simple to create. To create an apparently simple outcome the designer usually needs to have a comprehensive understanding of their craft and the requirements of their audience. When you look at a seemingly effortless creation it's worth thinking about the skill and hard work that went into making it look so easy.

In order for a visual story to be easily read by a third party it is important to consider the core messages that need to be conveyed and the most appropriate way to convey them. It is not always necessary to detail everything that needs to be said; however, it is important to know what parts of the story to control and which areas can be left for individual interpretation.

A simple visual note or expression that is able to capture the interest of an observer can be significantly more beneficial to understanding an overall message than any surplus detailing. The opening words of a story often aim to immediately intrigue and capture the attention of the audience, and a simple drawing should do the same. When the viewer immediately understands the basic message being conveyed their interest is usually secured, making them willing to delve further into the idea. Keep it simple, communicate clearly and adapt your visual story to suit the needs of its audience.

Communicate clearly

A clear analogy exists between spoken and visual communication. Just as with a written story, the communication of visual information needs to flow freely and avoid unnecessary complications. A logical journey needs to be created that can be followed and understood by the viewer. To clearly portray an idea, a sketch must include meaningful statements that guide the viewer with confidence.

A mark should not have to stutter along its intended pathway but should be able to move unchallenged and make an effective contribution to the visual story. A mark that struggles unnecessarily only manages to delay and complicate the message.

Shade
These 'sketched' pieces of furniture, hand drawn by Front, are like materialised illustrations. They are part of an ongoing exploration of where and when in the design process products start to exist in the real world. Exhibited at Spazio Rossana Orlandi.

Design
Front

Speaking visually

Absent-minded innovation > **Sketching** > Cross-discipline influences

Body text
Supplies an in-depth discussion of the topics covered.

Chapter navigation
Highlights the current chapter unit and lists previous and following units.

Visual conversations

Section sub-headings
Each section heading is
divided into sub-headings
to provide clear structure
and ease of navigation.

Boxed information
Provides supplementary
content in the form
of definitions, designer
biographies and
student exercises.

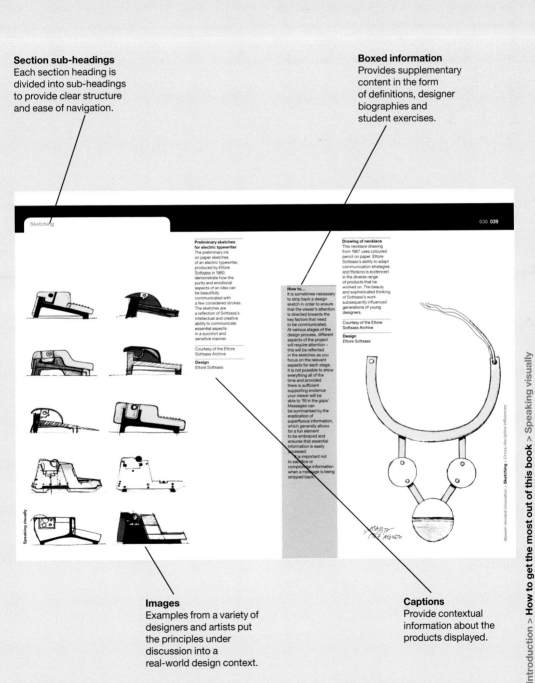

Sketching

038_039

**Preliminary sketches
for electric typewriter**
The preliminary ink
on paper sketches
of an electric typewriter,
produced by Ettore
Sottsass in 1960,
demonstrate how the
purity and emotional
aspects of an idea can
be beautifully
communicated with
a few considered strokes.
The sketches are
a reflection of Sottsass's
intellectual and creative
ability to communicate
essential aspects
in a succinct and
sensitive manner.

Courtesy of the Ettore
Sottsass Archive

Design
Ettore Sottsass

How to...
It is sometimes necessary
to strip back a design
sketch in order to ensure
that the viewer's attention
is directed towards the
key factors that need
to be communicated.
At various stages of the
design process, different
aspects of the project
will require attention –
this will be reflected
in the sketches as you
focus on the relevant
aspects for each stage.
It is not possible to show
everything all of the
time and provided
there is sufficient
supporting evidence
your viewer will be
able to 'fill in the gaps'.
Messages can
be summarised by the
eradication of
superfluous information,
which generally allows
for a fun element
to be embraced and
ensures that essential
information is easily
accessed.
It is important not
to sacrifice or
compromise information
when a message is being
stripped back.

Drawing of necklace
This necklace drawing
from 1967 uses coloured
pencil on paper. Ettore
Sottsass's ability to adapt
communication strategies
and thinking is evidenced
in the diverse range
of products that he
worked on. The beauty
and sophisticated thinking
of Sottsass's work
subsequently influenced
generations of young
designers.

Courtesy of the Ettore
Sottsass Archive

Design
Ettore Sottsass

Speaking visually

Absent-minded innovation > **Sketching** > Cross-discipline influences

Images
Examples from a variety of
designers and artists put
the principles under
discussion into a
real-world design context.

Captions
Provide contextual
information about the
products displayed.

Introduction > How to get the most out of this book > Speaking visually

The ability to communicate effectively and send accurate visual messages that can be readily understood by others is a fundamental function of design thinking.

It is essential to have an awareness and appreciation of the implied messages and stories that are being articulated by everyday marks and objects. The message transmitted by an object is usually the consequence of numerous minor characteristics and details managing to blend and work in harmony to form a cohesive statement to a particular target audience.

In this way, a product is not simply a form with a single function, but rather it is a collection of considered messages and agendas. It is an item that has been crafted and produced to perform in a particular fashion. For example, a product might demand a viewer's attention simply with bright colours or an unorthodox design, but once it has that attention it should be open to further investigation to reveal an array of meanings and narratives all working in conjunction with each other.

100% Make up – sketches
Expressive and simple sketches by Alessandro Mendini for the Alessi project 100% Make up.

Design
Alessandro Mendini
for Alessi
Alessi Spa,
Crusinallo, Italy

Inspiration

There are many different ways to prompt an initial idea and an array of subsequent methods that can be used to further nurture and refine it. It is important to remember that ideas exist in both a physical and mental state. Therefore, once you've identified an initial 'spark' of inspiration it should be possible to use a combination of imagination and physical prototypes to tease out lots of different options and suggestions to further develop your initial idea.

Be playful

The process of 'seeing an idea' is perhaps more akin to play than it is to work. This is because finding inspiration often involves developing a creative, somewhat chaotic, abstract or lateral mentality rather than a formal, ordered or literal approach. Creativity thrives when rules can be challenged and boundaries are broken in order to accommodate different ways of working.

For example, practices such as brainstorming and visual-storming can be very effective; these are techniques where a key word or image is used as a starting point to extract further responses from a selected, often eclectic audience. These processes can be extremely useful in opening up initial concepts. Similarly, an interactive role-play scenario is often useful in identifying and solving problems with ideas and prototypes.

The objects (and groups of objects) that surround us are also valuable in stimulating original ideas. It is not always necessary to visit museums, galleries and exhibitions to find inspiration; just looking, observing and absorbing the specific traits and peculiarities of everyday objects can be enough to trigger an idea. Objects are constantly speaking to us; suggesting opportunities and connections that we can choose to embrace, retain and reuse in our own work. We just need to learn their visual language.

Story drawing
This 'drawing story' or 'story map' explores the various narrative relationships that are often encountered in design. The selected letterforms manage to reflect meaning and are set out in a manner synonymous with natural thinking.

Design
Tim Donaldson

Speaking visually

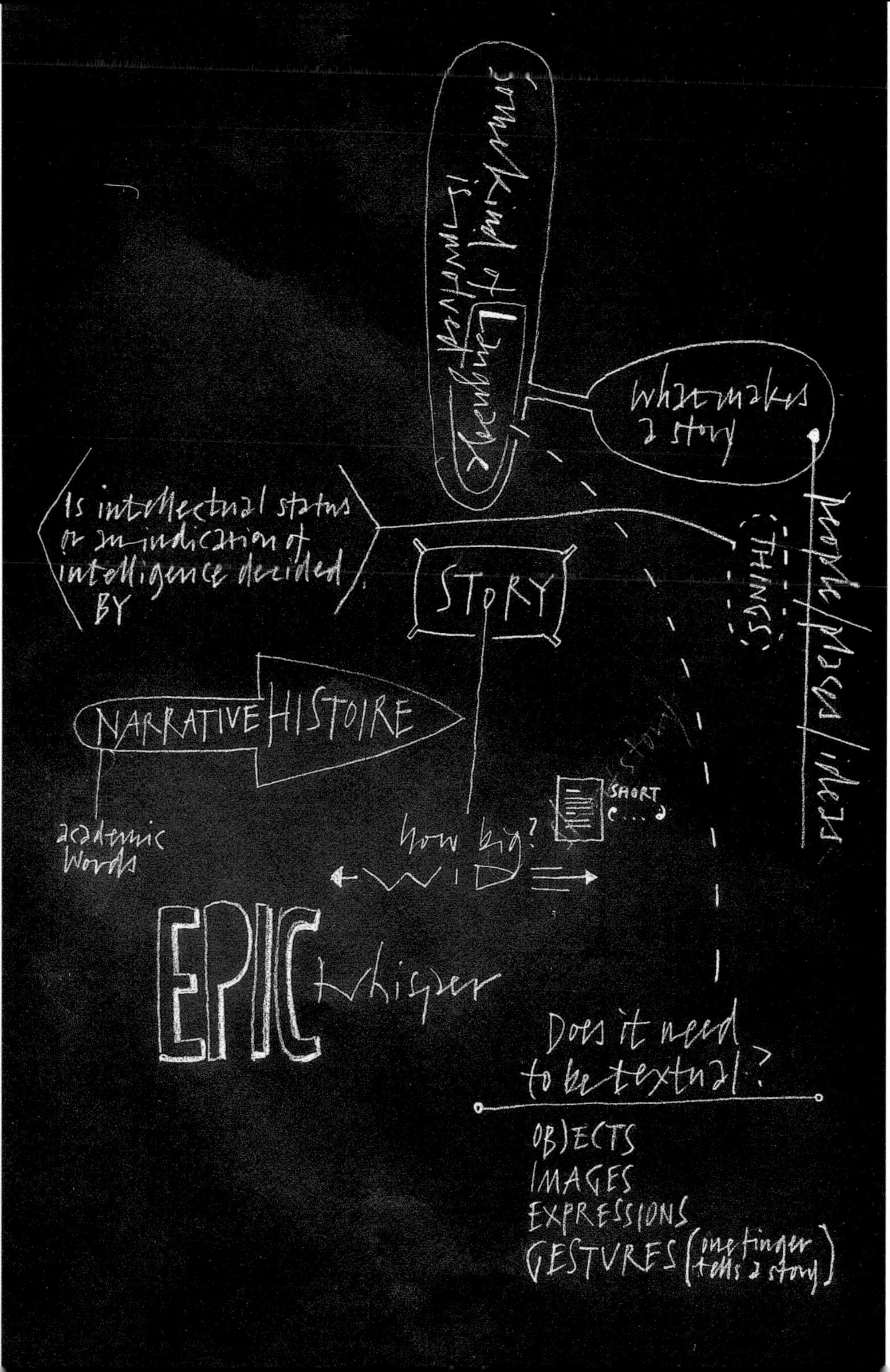

Some kind of language!

What makes a story

Is intellectual status or an indication of intelligence decided BY

STORY

THINGS

people/places/ideas

NARRATIVE HISTOIRE

academic Words

SHORT
[...]

how big?
← WIDE →

EPIC whisper

Does it need to be textual?

OBJECTS
IMAGES
EXPRESSIONS
GESTURES (one finger tells a story)

Mind maps

There are many different, visually creative methods for accessing new ideas and understanding their associated connections.

A particularly effective approach is the creation of a mind map. This is a process that can manage and organise visual and verbal references without any dominant bias. Creating a mind map does not require a formal or regimented approach (such as a schematic or a diagram might need) instead it aims to encourage the development of free, unrestrained thinking. The ability to formulate clear, tangible and simple associations frees the imagination and, although such maps might appear somewhat chaotic and random, they are a reflection of the thinking process. The creation of a mind map should involve an organic analysis that constantly reviews, questions and evolves – taking new ideas forward.

As a mind map does not necessarily follow any rigid rules it can be constructed in a very personal and unique manner. Although a fundamental and common strand may be evident, a map generally represents freedom of expression and interpretation. This means that it can sometimes be difficult for a third party to accurately decipher all of the information contained within a map. However, even a partial understanding is usually sufficient to grasp the core messages and meanings. Interpretation in this sense is similar to a standard conversation where gaps have to be filled and interpretations are made according to personal experiences.

Many leading design organisations embrace the idea of the mind map to stimulate thinking and understanding. Mind maps are often used in conjunction with other communicative methods, although approaches are also tailored to particular requirements. As Ravi Sawhney, founder and CEO of RKS describes: 'Mind mapping is extremely valuable to us because, as designers, "We know it when we see it". Mind mapping is a visual way for us to explore lines and possibilities and trigger visuals, even if only in our minds, that can lead us to a path for exploration and potential success. It also allows us to leave no stone unturned by which we could otherwise miss a great opportunity. Once a map is built, it triggers our visual thinking and allows us to pull in others and spark their creativity and brainstorming and go further and deeper than ever before.'

'The range of skills available to all of us include those previously attributed to either the left or right hemisphere:

1 Language: Words; Symbols

2 Number

3 Logic: Sequence, Listing; Linearity; Analysis; Time; Association

4 Rhythm

5 Colour

6 Imagery: Daydreaming; Visualisation

7 Spatial awareness: Dimension; Gestalt (whole picture)

Radiant thinking and mind mapping take all these elements into account.'

The Mind Map® Book, by kind permission of Tony Buzan. www.buzanworld.com

How to...
The approach to constructing a mind map usually begins with a central theme or a core idea, which may take the form of text or visuals, or a combination of both. As ideas and thoughts evolve, an organic, coloured structure emerges, developing necessary bridges and stimulating connections. The sensory journey is able to wander and evolve in any direction and is not overly constrained or governed. In this way, subconscious thoughts are brought to the fore and can be openly discussed and appraised.

Inspiration > Absent-minded innovation

Role play

Acting out a situation and adopting viewpoints and characteristics that you would not normally display can be enlightening. This kind of 'pretend activity' allows for inhibitions and conventional thinking to be put to one side for a period while alternative views are freely expressed. Temporarily arguing for another person's point-of-view allows a designer to view a problem from a different perspective. It also allows for any personal bias to be set aside so that ideas that may otherwise be relegated to the sidelines can take centre stage. It is fundamental to the success of a project that a diverse range of issues are explored and that both the negatives and the positives are challenged.

Many different techniques have been devised to encourage this kind of rigorous thinking. One of the most successful is the 'six thinking hats' approach devised by Dr Edward de Bono (www.edwdebono.com), who is a leading authority on creative thinking. The six-thinking-hats method uses coloured hats as metaphors for the different key stages of the creative thinking process. This technique is designed to help structure and develop group discussion and individual critical thinking by focusing on five distinct ways of thinking (and one overarching viewpoint).

The hats are worn either literally or figuratively to represent the point of view currently being used by that individual or member of the group. Adopting different personas and acting out different scenarios in this way allows for alternative experiences to be encountered, expressed and evaluated. Play is an important feature in the communication of messages and by capturing the imagination of the participants the whole process becomes more engaging. The different colours and states are:

- **White** signifies honesty and purity. The white hat represents the facts.

- **Red** signifies emotion and feelings. The red hat invites passion and expression.

- **Black** signifies caution and judgement. The black hat represents the negatives to be considered.

- **Yellow** signifies opportunity and forward thinking. The yellow hat is positive.

- **Green** signifies creativity and investigation. The green hat presents alternative options and proposals.

- **Blue** is the control colour, which ensures that all areas are represented fairly.

'The purpose of using mind maps, or any other visual mapping tool, is to cluster abstract data-points obtained from research, and discover relationships in the data. A designer is typically a dynamic visual worker whose process constantly changes and morphs. Mind maps help to channel this creative drive into pointed solutions relevant to the specific user context.'

Eric Chan, president of ECCO Design, New York

Affinity clusters

Hillary Carey, human factors researcher at IDEO, has conducted an analysis into the communication of ideas and the fundamental advantages behind the clustering of 'stickies': a process that IDEO refers to as 'affinity clusters'. At IDEO they consider the 'Post-it' note as an invaluable tool, and as Hillary describes, they are:

■ **Collaborative**
Because they are easily accessible, everyone can write Post-its together. Everyone captures and contributes their ideas, not just the person with the computer or the loudest voice.

■ **Shareable**
Because they are physical and visible on a wall, they are shareable. Everyone has access to the information on them and can easily read and add to the content.

■ **Rough and rapid**
Because they are cheap, the ideas on them are prototypes, ready to be changed and evolved as you learn more.

■ **Clusterable**
Because they are repositionable, the ideas are flexible, not fixed, so they can be grouped again and again, for synthesis, frameworks and voting.

■ **To the point**
Because they are small, they force people to be concise and pointed with their ideas, which helps team members understand the information quickly.

■ **More than words**
Because they aren't lined, they encourage small drawings, symbols and frameworks that help people communicate ideas differently.

Inspiration > Absent-minded innovation

How to...
Simple approaches to stimulating ideas and thoughts include brainstorming, visual-storming and role-play scenarios. All of these activities have an element of play and are therefore valuable in capturing a particular feeling or understanding a thought. Brainstorming and visual-storming sessions rely on assembling a group of individuals, often with contracting or diverse backgrounds, and instigating an activity where multiple and varied suggestions are generated in response to a primary trigger. In brainstorming sessions, it is usual for respondents to identify literal and lateral words related to their own experiences or feelings. Visual-storming adopts a similar agenda, however respondents use simple images that they create to suggest directions or ideas. Role play can be conducted independently or within a group and simply involves acting out the basic premise of an idea and its ensuing evaluation.

Chest of drawers
'The chest is a metaphor for the memory system. The Chest of Drawers is a collection of picked up drawers that have been given a new enclosure. These are then piled up on each other and held together with a furniture moving strap.'
Tejo Remy

Design
Tejo Remy for Droog

Photography
Robaard and Theuwkens / Marjo Kranenborg, CMK

REGENT'S
UNIVERSITY LONDON

Absent-minded innovation

Designers are not the only people with innovative ideas for their products. How many times have you seen a pen used to stir coffee, or a wall being used as a temporary seat or even a wire fence with litter squashed into its framework? These absent-minded improvisations can suggest new ideas for everyday objects.

Visual slang

Products are often used in ways that their designers never envisioned. Unfortunately, these new uses often go unnoticed as it is very easy to miss what is going on around us (even when we believe we are concentrating). Everyday processes, actions and movements become automatic so that relevant and inspirational ideas pass us by. However, paying attention to these improvised solutions to common problems can be highly illuminating.

Indeed, the strange and wonderful hybrids that emerge from the casual bastardisation of products generates an original language; a visual slang that has something worthwhile to say. Not only can these improvisations invite new ideas, they can also guide us to adjust a product in order to avoid continual abuse or misuse. A user's thoughtless adjustments to a product can be both amusing and disrespectful; however, such practical abbreviations and adaptations manage to demonstrate an ongoing metamorphosis of the visual language. Although changes that are thrust upon objects may appear to be a demonstration of ignorance, a form of visual illiteracy by the user, it is important to constantly observe the ways in which products are used in the real world.

Improvisation
A roadside post makes a convenient flag pole.
This kind of simple improvisation can provide an insight into people's requirements.

Adapted products in Shanghai

It is not always possible to predict how users will interact with a product and the use of electricity cables in Shanghai, China, to hang clothes may well surprise the cable's designers. However, it is something that should be considered in future design work to ensure public safety. Similarly, the use of a bicycle basket as a wastepaper basket may indicate a need for more street rubbish bins.

Photography
Tim Harrison

Sketching

An initial, momentary mark produced in an attempt to envisage and simply relay an idea should be carefully considered and expressed. Functional communication is a key objective in design and can adopt many different characteristics and personas. It is not just about the accurate and physical portrayal of something, which in isolation can often appear sterile, but also the emotional aspect and feeling that needs to be clearly represented.

Experiment

Impressions need to be controlled in a manner that is appropriate to the overall story and it is important to set a suitable context. It is necessary to experiment, explore and understand the different approaches to generating marks and to appreciate that the seemingly juxtaposed elements of freedom of expression and practical constraint can actually be complementary features and not opposing forces within our work. It can be important to occasionally move away from comfort zones and try alternative and innovative methods to create a visual language, and ascertain the most suitable tools for the journey. Investigating peripheral approaches and those usually employed within other disciplines can often provide an insight about how a mark could be controlled and exploited.

A moth to a flame
The dynamism of a moth attracted to a light is beautifully captured and recorded without unnecessary information being evident. The spiral path that is tracked by the moth is faithfully replicated in the subsequent physical form.

Design
Todd Bracher, Efe Buluc and Mark Goetz for to22

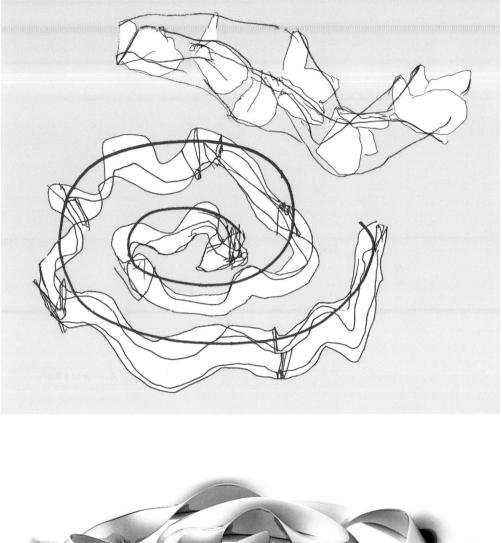

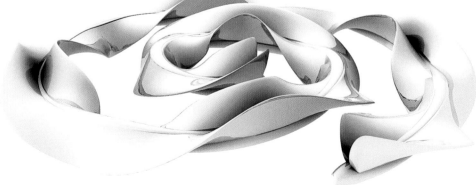

> 'And the first rude sketch that the world had seen was joy to his mighty heart, till the Devil whispered behind the leaves "It's pretty, but is it Art?"'
>
> **Rudyard Kipling, author and poet**

Make it clear and engaging

The movement and nature of a sketch (the way in which it twists and turns) needs to be executed in a way that excites to ensure that a certain energy and life is captured. Inaccurate sketches, created without a clear idea of what needs to be communicated, can only cause confusion. However, a simple, well-executed mark has the potential to communicate an incredible range of languages with sensitivity and elegance. The careful and comprehensive control of different tools will allow something that may otherwise be visually mundane to suddenly assume life and character. A visual message, like a story, can be told very simply and eloquently without the need for any unnecessary embellishments.

The techniques and marks employed in portraying a concept may change and evolve as additional information becomes available and the idea becomes more substantial. However, whatever the method of communication, the message should always be clear, uncluttered and capture the imagination of the viewer.

Allo?!
The beautifully simple and effective drawings shown opposite capture the essence of the 'Allo?!' entryphone above. The design is based on the idea of the cup and string telephones used by children. The purity and confidence in the visual communication suitably reflects the characteristic of the product and the story.

Design
Guillaume Delvigne, Ionna Vautrin for Industreal®.
All rights reserved.

Photography
Ilvio Gallo

Speaking visually

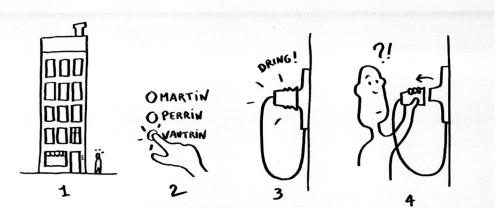

'A sketch is generally more spirited than a picture.'
Denis Diderot, philosopher, art critic and writer

Keeping it simple

A simple design is often anything but simple to create. To create an apparently simple outcome the designer usually needs to have a comprehensive understanding of their craft and the requirements of their audience. When you look at a seemingly effortless creation it's worth thinking about the skill and hard work that went into making it look so easy.

In order for a visual story to be easily read by a third party it is important to consider the core messages that need to be conveyed and the most appropriate way to convey them. It is not always necessary to detail everything that needs to be said; however, it is important to know what parts of the story to control and which areas can be left for individual interpretation.

A simple visual note or expression that is able to capture the interest of an observer can be significantly more beneficial to understanding an overall message than any surplus detailing. The opening words of a story often aim to immediately intrigue and capture the attention of the audience, and a simple drawing should do the same. When the viewer immediately understands the basic message being conveyed their interest is usually secured, making them willing to delve further into the idea. Keep it simple, communicate clearly and adapt your visual story to suit the needs of its audience.

Communicate clearly

A clear analogy exists between spoken and visual communication. Just as with a written story, the communication of visual information needs to flow freely and avoid unnecessary complications. A logical journey needs to be created that can be followed and understood by the viewer. To clearly portray an idea, a sketch must include meaningful statements that guide the viewer with confidence.

A mark should not have to stutter along its intended pathway but should be able to move unchallenged and make an effective contribution to the visual story. A mark that struggles unnecessarily only manages to delay and complicate the message.

Speaking visually

Shade

These 'sketched' pieces of furniture, hand drawn by Front, are like materialised illustrations. They are part of an ongoing exploration of where and when in the design process products start to exist in the real world. Exhibited at Spazio Rossana Orlandi.

Design

Front

'I didn't want to approach AQ as a bathroom collection. Everything is so white, so clinical. And it's a room hidden from everyone. Why not treat it as furniture?'

Jaime Hayón, artist-designer

Capturing ideas

An idea is usually an ephemeral experience and something that often needs to be quickly captured, and translated before it is lost. Even if an idea initially appears vague, if it can be captured then it can rapidly mature and be physically communicated as a viable proposition. Ultimately, a design thinking process will explore and develop possible options, so the initial representation only needs to be an impression and nothing else.
The construction of the image needs to have commitment and strength, but it does not need to be perfect. Amendments in the physical way that something is communicated can, if necessary, be resolved although this is not always needed or desired. A sterile and emotionless image is often characterless and can be less inspiring than something that has an element of misrepresentation, energy or intrigue.

Sketches of the AQHayon bathroom collection
The sketches by the inspirational Spanish designer, Jaime Hayón, capture the alluring mood and theatrical presence of the AQHayon 'bathroom' collection. An organic and free-flowing language manages to challenge convention and is faithfully transposed into the bathroom 'furniture'.

Design
Jaime Hayón

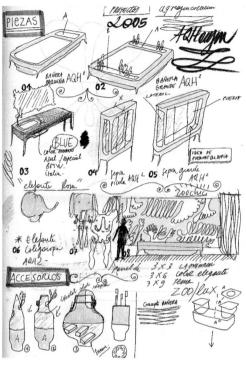

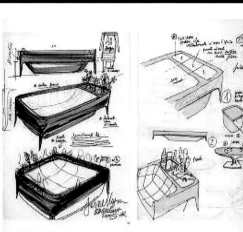

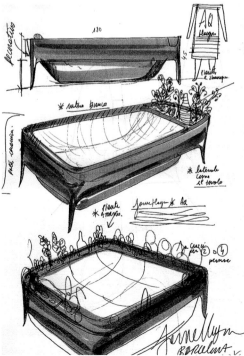

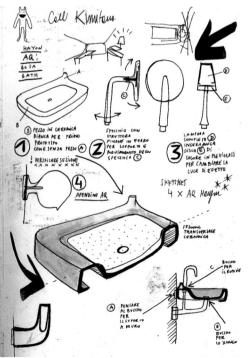

> 'I've always drawn. Through drawing, I got into building things I would contemplate and sketch out shapes in my head.'
>
> **Bruce Bulger, custom woodworker and fine artist**

Keeping an observational journal

Various styles and scenarios can be evident within an observational journal as it is in essence a personal discussion of how things are or could be perceived, and it should therefore be as imaginative as possible. Continually observing and recording ideas, feelings and possibilities in response to an identified problem in the form of simple visual notes and limited annotation can be a highly useful tactic. These notes should not be restricted to a particular genre or style, but should be free to cross boundaries depending on the clarity of information required and the level of detail that is deemed appropriate. A varied, even apparently chaotic approach to recording and portraying ideas can frequently aid creative thinking as the different associations trigger new possibilities. Sketched or scribbled ideas and suggestions should complement and interact with each other rather than appear as regimented and isolated notes. The ensuing assembly of ideas is often assisted with colour and other relevant references such as scale and texture.

AQHayon bathroom collection
The beautiful finished products perfectly reflect the inspiration of the developmental sketches shown on the previous pages.

Design
Jaime Hayón

How to...

It is extremely useful to keep an observational journal, sketchbook or visual diary close to hand to help identify and develop new ideas. Simple sketches, accompanied by brief notes to emphasise different possibilities, will enable an idea to progress freely. The drawings need to communicate information effectively but can still be quick and loose. The images do not need to be overworked. Initial sketches help to tell the overall story of a product's development and even if you reject the sketched ideas later it is still worth keeping them to help keep track of the project's progress.

Absent-minded innovation > **Sketching** > Cross-discipline influences

Purity

An attitude that allows for an enhanced freedom of interpretation and perhaps incorporates unfamiliar practices can occasionally be more meaningful than a more prescriptive, literal approach. A quick, unconstrained sketch can often be the best tool for depicting sensitive, vivacious ideas. An impressionist outlook, executed with a complete understanding of the information that needs to be conveyed, has the potential to capture the overall mood of the project and include small but important details that might otherwise be overlooked.

The function of a product is not restricted to an individual or dominant feature and likewise a sketch should avoid being predominantly concerned with a single issue. There is a significant amount of information that can and should be communicated in addition to the obvious, key features of the design.

Misrepresentation is not beneficial, but partial representation that provides an initial insight and invites discussion can be constructive. Poetic portrayals that recognise a relationship between the imagination and the physical can engage the senses and avoid a project being forced down a rigid, formal development path too soon. A relaxed, graceful approach where messages are undefined and boundaries merge can provide the opportunity for a design story to gently unfold with scope for any realistic translation to be explored at a subsequent stage.

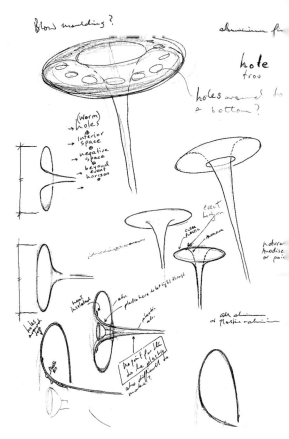

Helice lamp sketches
In these initial sketches by Marc Newson, which were produced during the development of the beautiful Helice lamp for FLOS, personal and technical observations complement the purity and elegance of the product.

Design
Marc Newson for FLOS

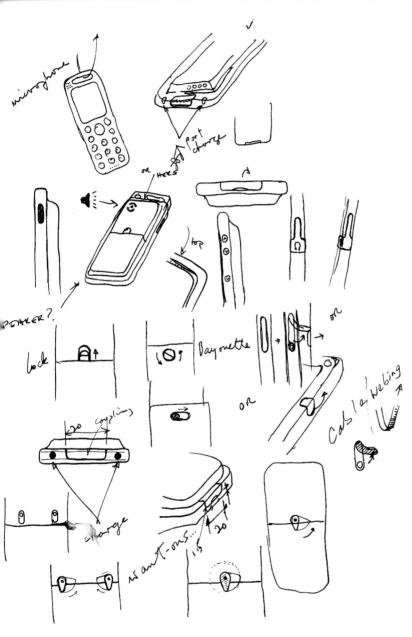

Talby mobile phone sketches
The careful consideration of detail and the different options for the phone designs are effectively expressed and explored in these sketches. At the same time, the sketches also capture a vibrancy and innocence that is evident in the eventual KDDI product.

Design
Marc Newson
for KDDI Japan

Dedicato Alla Letteratura/Dedicated to Literature

The simplistic beauty and warmth of the solid cherry is adequately communicated through a partial impression using watercolour. The soft language of the object merges to portray an appealing and sensory message.

Design

Michele De Lucchi and Mario Rossi Scola. Produced by Design Gallery

Photography

Tom Vack

How to...

It is important to continually experiment with different tools for generating marks; try to mix and match various techniques to assess exactly what works best for each design. An investigation into the work of other designers and other disciplines, as well as research, into historical techniques, can offer inspiration on a whole range of diverse tools. Mark-making tools are everywhere and can be found or crafted to generate particular impressions. While it is important to know and master traditional approaches it is also beneficial to challenge them with improvisation. A visit to a gallery or museum will provide an opportunity to be introduced to unfamiliar applications.

Speaking visually

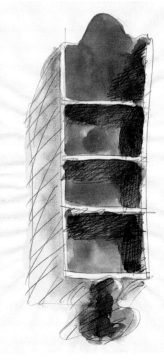

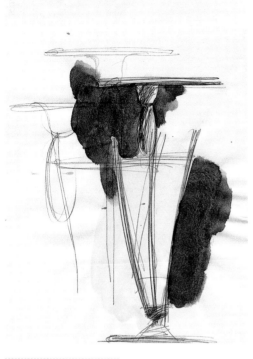

**Dedicato All'ospitalita/
Dedicated to Hospitality**
An impression of the solid
cherry wood cloak stand
is sufficiently expressed
by Michele De Lucchi
using a few confident and
carefully chosen strokes.
The base of the stand
is decorated using plastic
laminate.

Design
Michele De Lucchi
and Mario Rossi Scola.
Produced by
Design Gallery

Photography
Tom Vack

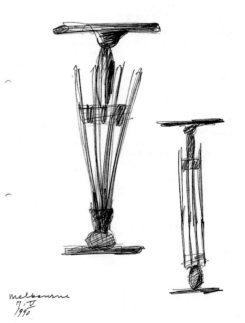

Melbourne
7.V
1990

**Preliminary sketches
for electric typewriter**
The preliminary ink
on paper sketches
of an electric typewriter,
produced by Ettore
Sottsass in 1960,
demonstrate how the
purity and emotional
aspects of an idea can
be beautifully
communicated with
a few considered strokes.
The sketches are
a reflection of Sottsass's
intellectual and creative
ability to communicate
essential aspects
in a succinct and
sensitive manner.

Courtesy of the Ettore
Sottsass Archive

Design
Ettore Sottsass

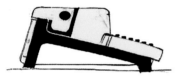

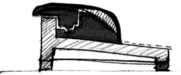

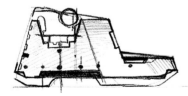
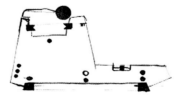

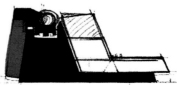

Speaking visually

How to…

It is sometimes necessary to strip back a design sketch in order to ensure that the viewer's attention is directed towards the key factors that need to be communicated. At various stages of the design process, different aspects of the project will require attention – this will be reflected in the sketches as you focus on the relevant aspects for each stage. It is not possible to show everything all of the time and provided there is sufficient supporting evidence your viewer will be able to 'fill in the gaps'. Messages can be summarised by the eradication of superfluous information, which generally allows for a fun element to be embraced and ensures that essential information is easily accessed.

It is important not to sacrifice or compromise information when a message is being stripped back.

Drawing of necklace
This necklace drawing from 1967 uses coloured pencil on paper. Ettore Sottsass's ability to adapt communication strategies and thinking is evidenced in the diverse range of products that he worked on. The beauty and sophisticated thinking of Sottsass's work subsequently influenced generations of young designers.

Courtesy of the Ettore Sottsass Archive

Design
Ettore Sottsass

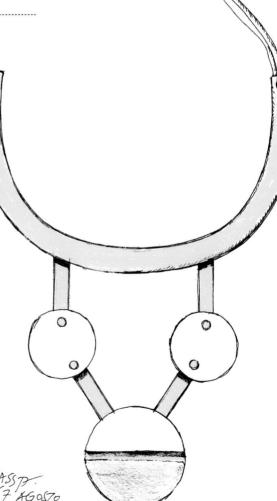

Cross-discipline influences

It is important to remain inquisitive and receptive to unfamiliar design practices in order to continually broaden creative horizons. By incorporating approaches and techniques typically used by other subject areas (such as architecture or fashion design) into design work it is possible to introduce new opportunities and prevent the development of a bland, uninventive working environment.

Finding inspiration

Seeking out an unusual method of manipulation or working with a new material can suggest interesting new directions for us as designers. Reading articles from unfamiliar journals, allowing the imagination to be challenged with visionary writings and attending creative exhibitions and workshops from other design disciplines can lead to a whole new world of inspiration. The ability to converse confidently with different visual languages is something that evolves through curiosity and interaction; it is an ongoing and fundamental process of learning and development.

Understanding contemporary approaches to visual communication and the many different ways in which different disciplines convey crucial messages is clearly useful. However, it is equally important to appreciate historical approaches and thereby develop an awareness of how design narratives have evolved over the years. Successful designers often manage to be visually conversant in a number of disciplines, from a number of historical periods, and are therefore able to adjust according to the demands of a whole range of projects and clients.

The 'Libri' cabinet
Piero Fornasetti was a prolific and highly creative sculptor, artist and craftsman.
He created an incredibly diverse range of beautiful work, which successfully combined disciplines and transcended cultures.

Design
Piero Fornasetti

Image
© Barnaba Fornasetti

Speaking visually

**Piero Fornasetti
(1913–1988)**
Piero Fornasetti was
a skilled self-taught artist
who was able to merge
disciplines and transpose
imaginative and
architectural imagery
onto a fantastic array
of products. He gained
inspiration from
observations,
photographs and
journals. He also
benefited from a fruitful
association with the
founder of *Domus*
magazine, Giovanni
Ponti, who in 1940
ensured that many of
Fornasetti's designs were
featured in the
internationally acclaimed
journal. The collaboration
between Gio Ponti and
Piero Fornasetti
developed and they
subsequently embarked
on a series of creative
and detailed works.
    Piero Fornasetti's son,
Barnaba Fornasetti, has
successfully continued
the prolific and
stimulating approach
of his inspirational father
with visually
sophisticated works
such as 'Kiss'.

The 'Kiss' cabinet
The 'Kiss' cabinet was
created in 2007
as a limited edition piece
for Nilufar. It takes the
form of the 1950s cabinet
'Libri' designed
by Barnaba Fornasetti's
father, Piero Fornasetti.
The striking image
of the lips is inspired
by the Fornasetti series
Tema e Variazioni.

Design
Barnaba Fornasetti

Image
© Barnaba Fornasetti

Sketching > Cross-discipline influences

'Our intention is to capture the spontaneity and power of a sketch and present it as a three-dimensional object.'

to22

Linear to physical

Moving on from two-dimensional sketches to create three-dimensional structures helps us to extend our thinking from the linear to the physical. It also helps us to identify and focus on the key messages that need to be conveyed. This can be achieved using very loose physical prototypes, which can be controlled in a similar way to a sketch.

Just as with a two-dimensional sketch, a loose prototype can suggest a basic message, but it is other elements such as the colour and texture that really tell the story. A swathe of colour, even if it is roughly placed, is able to generate a response from an observer and assist with meaning.

Assembling physical ideas and recognising potential through efficient decision making is very similar to drawing; if it is conducted well, then it should be very intuitive. Physical sketches generated with care and sensitivity can communicate messages that confront and challenge the observer. It is also possible to construct representations of an idea using a chaotic and seemingly abstract approach that may ultimately appear subdued and tranquil. The physical manipulation of spatial marks intrigues the imagination and allows for a constant stream of sculpted ideas to be evaluated.

How to...
The 'T' system is a popular approach to creative design. This system requires an individual to be primarily focused on a particular area of design (symbolised by the shaft of the 'T'). However, they must also look sideways at other disciplines to appreciate the approaches and attitudes of others (symbolised by the horizontal bar of the 'T'). In this way, creative designers encourage the interaction of different design teams and researchers to address a particular problem rather than rely on a single subject strand. Interaction and dialogue stimulate thinking.

Speaking visually

The conception project
The conception project
manages to capture
the freedom
and expressive nature
of an initial sketch and
transpose its honest
qualities into a physical
form. The delicate and
fragile language
of the sketch is echoed
in steel.

Design
Todd Bracher, Efe Buluc
and Mark Goetz for to22

Drawing is addictive, and as such it is something that all designers are constantly engaged with and feel compelled to work at and explore. It is common to produce dozens of drawings for a single project; most of these sketches will never be seen by anyone else but still constitute vital elements in the design process.

The constraints of any given sketching medium can often force a design to take an exciting or unexpected direction. For this reason, many designers use their drawing as a thinking process; a private experience where emotions and feelings can be expressed. It is often the process rather than the outcome that captures the imagination and moves a project forward.

The specific traits of an emotional drawing or product may not ultimately be perceived by the viewer in exactly the way that the artist or designer intended. However, the overall message is usually effectively communicated. The manipulation of a product to generate a reaction within a user is an important function and an area that requires careful consideration and appraisal.

Renault Fiftie
In 1996 the Renault Fiftie concept was lovingly created to celebrate the 50th anniversary of the Renault 4CV. The honest and pure language of the Renault Fiftie manages to creatively combine contrasting elements with sophistication and beauty. Emotions are entertained through charming and delightful features, such as the twisted ribbon-styled lights and the natural tactility of the interior space.

Courtesy of Renault Corporate Communications

Design
Renault

Emotional responses > Seeing the gap

Emotional thinking

'By emphasising how we interact with robots this project introduces a very different way of thinking about what robots might look like, how they will fit into our lives, and the psychological aspects of our interactions with them.'

Anthony Dunne, designer

Expressive creativity

The application of emotional thinking, or expressive creativity, during the physical development of a product allows designers the freedom to nurture and explore different options. The emotional process can successfully embrace unfamiliar directions and confront taboos since the approach relies on instincts rather than logic to stimulate the emergence of new ideas.

**Anthony Dunne and
Fiona Raby**
Dunne and Raby are
interactive product
designers who research
design thinking through
a process that combines
elements of theory with
practical enquiry.
The approach aims
to identify the potential
directions of emerging
technology and
anticipate user
interaction. The
Technological Dreams
Series: No.1, Robots
created in 2007
explores possible
personas attached
to 'technological
cohabitants'. Animated
characteristics and
behaviours are adopted
by the collection.

**Technological Dreams
Series: No. 1, Robots**
'This project offers
a suggested insight into
our future interaction with
intelligent machines.
It considers the different
interdependencies and
relationships that might
emerge in relation to
different levels of robot
intelligence and capability.
These objects are meant
to spark a discussion
about how we'd like our
robots to relate to us:
subservient, intimate,
dependent or equal?'
Dunne and Raby

Design
Anthony Dunne and
Fiona Raby

Photography
Per Tingleff

Emotional thinking > Energy and passion

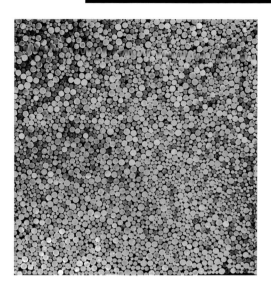

Understanding

A completed object that has evolved through an understanding of emotional expression can be visually comfortable but it does not need to be overly refined. It is usually the overall emotional message and not the individual statements or component details that make an impression.

The ability to think conceptually and use personal experiences and feelings allows a diverse range of product relationships to be explored and for innovative, exciting and unexpected outcomes to be revealed. In addition to the specific item being designed, an emotional approach is also able to appreciate and comprehend the space that it physically inhabits, and recognises that this also needs to be considered rather than being overlooked or regarded as an isolated feature.

I Like Grass and Living in the Clouds
The naturally beautiful installations I Like Grass and Living in the Clouds were exhibited at the Milan Furniture Fair 2008. They manage to successfully merge reality and belief to create an intuitive situation that, as the designers describe: '…blurs the lines between the ins and the outs, what's imaginary and what's not'.

Design
Valentina Audrito and Abhishake Kumbhat

Emotional responses

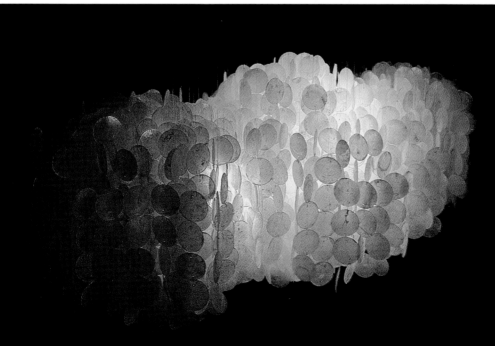

Emotional thinking > Energy and passion

Intuition

A visceral approach to creative thinking that relies on instinct and belief rather than theory allows designs to develop in a pure and uncomplicated way. Design intuition is an innate ability to connect with an idea and comfortably develop it down a particular pathway. This natural gift can be further developed through experience and encouraged to become a truly valuable resource.

An intuitive understanding is a demonstration of empathy, where an ability to offer simple, spontaneous solutions from subconscious references demonstrates natural awareness. This instant understanding should be transferred to the end user in order to promote clear interaction with the end product. A target audience should be comfortable and able to intuitively read the language of a product without any unnecessary complications.

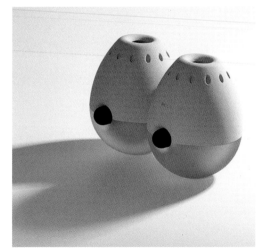

Emotional containers
An understanding
of emotions and the
preciousness of objects
were embraced by Philips
in 1995 with a range
of proposed Emotional
containers.
The cherished, sculptural
forms, guardians
of sensory messages,
adopt a sophisticated
persona. The sensory
holders dispense
fragrance, images
and sound.

Design
Philips Design

Emotional thinking > Energy and passion

'The Kalashnikov is light, functional, reliable, affordable and elegant; with more than 100 million copies officially produced it's one of the greatest hits of industrial design for this generation. Mr Kalashnikov doesn't get any royalties. He often complains about it. I will therefore give him a share of the benefits made on the sale of a representation of his model. Poor man. The rest will be given to MSF international. I wonder why. To tears citizens. To arms citizens.'

Philippe Starck, product designer

Sensory appeals

Most people form attachments to objects and products that, to an outsider, might seem irrational or even perverse. When there is a sentimental connection between an individual and an object, a personal attachment is formed that often defies conventional logic. If a product stirs up memories of a particular experience, then it can often trigger a whole range of senses and feelings. Passion, love, desire and worship are tags attached to products where a particular bond has been expressed.

An emotional response to a product can be instigated by an individual feature or through the composition of different elements. The texture, scent, sound or morphology of a particular item can charm and create a feel-good sensation. The personal associations to experiences and individual reactions vary considerably. However, products can be conditioned to send out particular signals and aim to capture the attention of a responsive audience.

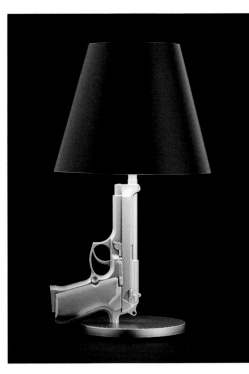

Table Gun Light and Bedside Gun Light
These 18-carat gold-plated lights demand attention by provoking feelings and emotions. As Philippe Starck explains: 'The gold on the guns represents the collusion of money and war. 'Table Gun' represents the East. 'Bed Side Gun' represents Europe. 'Lounge Gun' represents the West. The black lampshade represents Death. The crosses inside remind us of our dead.'

Courtesy Starck Network

Design
Philippe Starck for FLOS

Emotional thinking > Energy and passion

Causing confusion

An object can also be configured to be deliberately vague and even misleading. This design 'deceit' can intentionally lure the observer into an inappropriate reaction. This approach can help in grabbing a viewer's attention by creating a sense of curiosity in order to communicate a much more meaningful message on further investigation.

Similarly designs may be constructed in such a way as to imitate the materials and processes of more expensive or prestigious products – this is especially common when aesthetic judgement is a predominant feature of the end-user's decision. If a designed object appears too ordinary and does not demonstrate any exciting or intriguing characteristic then it can be very difficult for it to get noticed. Decisions and subconscious visual assessments are conducted in an instant and the immediate impression transmitted by a design is often critical. The adoption of an unexpected and unconventional visual dialogue can make something seem interesting enough to warrant further investigation.

Mixed messages

A viewer's initial response to an object may not always be what the designer expects as visual signals can be easily misconstrued. The development of a product can often be long and complicated, with obscure references and themes woven into the end result. In this way, if a third party is not familiar with the background of an object the message being projected can easily be misread and misunderstood. To help avoid unintentional confusion it is worthwhile showing new designs to friends and colleagues and asking them to explain their impressions. If they haven't perceived what the design is intended to convey then it may be necessary to revisit and clarify the design.

Layers of interest

A product, like a piece of literature, can be read and understood. Like a book, a product can also be interpreted in different ways and a closer examination can reveal detail that may not have been immediately obvious. If fragments of additional information about a product can be identified at later stages and a bigger picture understood by delving deep, additional layers of information can assist in retaining user interest.

The manipulation of a visual language to conceal an underlying message enables a seemingly simple story to be rejuvenated with new information and insight.

How to…
To understand the requirements of the design process it is important to consider why certain object relationships, compositions and characteristics have been created and why they have a certain appeal. Being constantly aware and making mental notes of detail, compositions and relationships of existing designs provides a catalogue of information that will help in predicting how users will relate to future designs.

The Olivetti Valentine typewriter
The attractive, red typewriter was designed in 1969 as an accessory, something different and imaginative, a passionate product that might inspire creativity in the user.

Design
Ettore Sottsass and Perry King

Emotional thinking > Energy and passion

Energy and passion

Using unconventional drawing techniques that demonstrate more energy and passion than traditional technical sketches can provoke a strong emotional reaction in the creator and the observer. Departing from familiar, anticipated protocols during the initial communication stages can provide an opportunity to play with expression and emotional meaning.

Multiple meanings

A drawing does not need to be a literal representation of an object. It does not need to be clinical or characterless. A design drawing, like a piece of art, has the capacity to communicate the spirit and essence of the object by focusing on a particular attribute or an associated reference in order to tell a story.

There is often a misconception that a designed object only has a single function, when quite the opposite is true. A well-conceived design operates on multiple levels and demonstrates multiple physical and psychological attributes. A drawing has the same potential; it is a vehicle to portray multiple stories and meanings.

The development of a design is an ongoing process with new ideas and information constantly dictating the direction to be taken. A substantial amount of background understanding is acquired in advance of the creative stages being put into practice; key decisions need to be made before a physical commitment is made. It is important to know what message needs to be told and the most effective approaches to be used to succeed.

Collage

A collage of visual artefacts and pictures composed to portray a particular mood or a desired attribute of a proposed design is a useful tool in encouraging new ideas. In this technique, direct references to an intended outcome are substituted for suggestion and emotional imagery. An emotional drawing can function in a similar fashion, where visual triggers can set the scene of a proposal without being too prescriptive.

**Emotional Sketches:
La Vuelta Desk and
Golf Fan**
These two sketches
manage to record the
sensory aspects
of the products rather
than concentrating
on their purely physical
attributes.

Design
King & Miranda Design

King & Miranda Design
Perry King and Santiago
Miranda offer expertise
across a wide range
of services, interiors and
product types. These
range from consumer
goods to furniture,
lighting and
telecommunications,
with expertise in
research and innovation
also playing a key role
in the company's
activities.

King & Miranda's
clients have included:
Akaba, Arteluce, Black
& Decker, Ericsson, Fiat,
FLOS, Olivetti, and Expo
'92 in Seville. They have
also been recognised
through awards, King
being elected as Royal
Designer for Industry
in 2000, Miranda winning
the *Premio Nacional de
Diseño* (Spanish
National Prize for Design)
in 1989 and the
Andalucian Prize for
Design in 1995.

Emotional thinking > **Energy and passion**

'Genuine poetry can communicate before it is understood.'
T. S. Eliot, poet, dramatist and literary critic

Poetry

Poetry can be an amalgamation of specific emotions, beliefs and experiences that are expressed in a cohesive and succinct form. A poem is eloquently composed and manages to communicate and rouse emotions. Poetry can also be an opportunity to explore, to question convention and communicate a poignant or underlying message without restrictions. Poetry has a freedom that might be seen as being innocent and pure, but it can also be intentionally abrupt and direct.

An object that is intelligently constructed with neighbouring elements reinforcing a cohesive message can demonstrate a harmony and fluidity that is often lacking in ill-considered designs. It is important to pay attention to all of the inherent details of a design; the sensory aspects and the perceptions that will ensure that other people will understand the intended message. A subtle misrepresentation or an ill-conceived marriage of visual triggers can inadvertently send out inappropriate messages, stories that belie the essence of the object.

The freedom to tell a story and manipulate visual similes and metaphors is an approach that can make impressionable connections. Poetry involves play, the teasing and chasing of different arrangements and the physical scripting of a thought. The message does not need to be strikingly obvious or brash but rather an accurate suggestion, something that allows some movement and retains some gaps for individual interpretation and imagination. The purpose of poetry in design is to enjoy the language.

How to…

Experimenting and combining a range of media, and understanding the innovative and effective approaches used by various designers throughout history reveals an infinite range of opportunities. Combinations such as ink and pastel, pencil and gouache or tempera and ink have been effectively employed for decades and should be revisited and evaluated now in the search for an empathetic process.

Designers from previous generations often demonstrated great visual ingenuity with what may be considered to be limited resources by contemporary standards.

Don't be afraid to adopt a technique just because it is not new or fashionable.

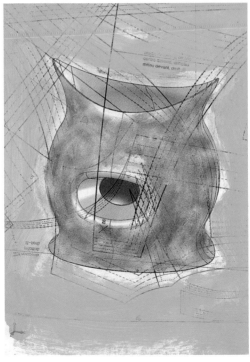

Emotional Sketches: Knossos Vase and Mitzy light fitting

These King & Miranda images successfully communicate lateral and inherent contexts rather than simply concentrating on literal messages. This imaginative and vibrant approach provides the observer with information that might not be captured with a more mundane process.

Design
King & Miranda Design

Mixed media

Using a combination of different media to communicate a particular element or feeling can be very effective. It is not always possible or desirable to capture the essence of something with a single visual facsimile, but a combination of different textures, references and approaches can provide an outcome that intrigues and stimulates emotions for further development.

By employing a whole range of media and allowing them to influence the direction of a project, new, unfamiliar opportunities can come to light. The controlled assembly of a visual message from a seemingly eclectic range of styles allows for depth, scale and form to be portrayed in a manner that would not otherwise be possible. Mixed-media approaches allow for accepted values to be challenged and can present an element of surprise.

Mixed media provides the opportunity to enjoy communication; it is a vacation from the ordinary and presents a strand of creativity that is both refreshing and informative. The chaotic nature that often ensues through the use of mixed media has an energy and vibrancy that is often absent in other forms of visual communication.

Construction

The application of interesting and unusual marks that might be somewhat unrestrained and digress from more familiar approaches presents the opportunity for absorbing and provocative stories to be told. Mixed media naturally invites an exploration of form, colour and texture using processes that may be unfamiliar.

Layering found materials or images and subsequently working over the surfaces can transform a message to mean something original, exciting and interesting. There is usually an abstract element to the use of mixed media that allows for outcomes to challenge preconceived thinking and inspire new ideas.

It is always worth considering mixed media as a means to communicate imaginatively and sensitively; it is the combination of art and design and has much to offer the creative process. Mixing techniques also helps us avoid habits – it can force us to leave our comfort zone. An intrepid attitude, a manner of thinking that is prepared to branch out and do something that seizes a particular opportunity, to say something differently, is usually constructive.

Collage *n*. a form of art in which various materials such as photographs and pieces of paper or fabric are arranged and stuck to a backing

Eclectic *adj*. deriving ideas, style or taste from a broad and diverse range of sources

**Emotional Sketches:
Moai light fitting**
In this image mixed media is used to communicate a sensual message.

Design
King & Miranda Design

Emotional thinking > **Energy and passion**

There is usually far more to a design than a superficial message and less obvious details can be discovered, and understood through direct interaction with the object. However, the audience's prior experience will determine how they read a particular message, meaning that subtle messages can be easily misunderstood if the designer has misjudged their audience's knowledge.

Conceptual themes are therefore fundamental to the development of a product from concept to reality. Themes allow designers to clearly identify and portray the essential indicators of their intended subject. These indicators provide a helpful framework for the viewer to easily understand the different messages and applications of the end product. To reach an intended design destination requires an understanding of the intended audience; what is it that makes them think the way they do and appreciate the issues that surround them? By understanding the audience it is possible to guide them to a full appreciation of the message being communicated.

This & That glass domes
This astonishing collection, which fuses glass bells with everyday objects, was designed by the inspirational designers at the Creative Lab of Fabrica, The Benetton Group Communications Research Center. The collection is based on an idea by American designer Tak Cheung and is produced by Secondome Edizioni.

Designer
Tak Cheung, Jade Folawiyo, Sam Baron, Catarina Carreiras, Valentina Carretta and Cristina Dias for Fabrica

----

Photography
Sebastiano Scattolin/ Fabrica

Emotional responses > **Seeing the gap** > Talking aesthetically

Stories

When an audience learns a new fact about the history or creation of an object it can completely change their perception of that object. If this new information, the story behind the product, is not widely known then the audience can feel a greater sense of attachment to the product; as though they've been given access to the designer's 'inner sanctum'.

Revealed meaning

Sparking a viewer's curiosity to intrigue them into finding out more about a design's development can lead a viewer to feel a heightened connection with the product – giving benefit to both the viewer and the design. A product is seen differently when additional information becomes available and any initial impressions may need to be amended. Stories and feelings that are subconsciously or consciously incorporated into the aesthetic make-up of a product may contain a whole range of messages that can significantly contrast with a viewer's first impression.

    The underlying message may simply be a theme that was never intended to be revealed or analysed but that, when discovered, can enhance a viewer's interest and emotions. The visual ambiguity that surrounds certain products has a chemistry that can be positively exploited. A passion for detail in design offers the opportunity for viewers to gradually discover different layers of meaning that can inform, fascinate and enchant.

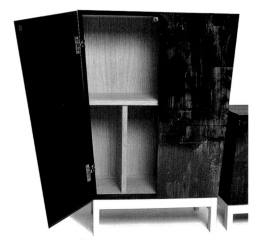

'Modus: cover is a cupboard distinguished by the fashion prevalent on the day it was built. It is reminiscent of the magical moment when renovating an old house and newspapers, as old as the house, are found behind the wallpaper.'

Fredrik Färg, designer

Modus: cover
Swedish designer Fredrik Färg's cupboard
is adorned with carefully selected images from fashion journals, a chic shroud that manages to capture and communicate the mood and style of the period when the item was constructed. The cupboard also contains a hidden, original journal that complements the outer surface.

Designer
Fredrik Färg

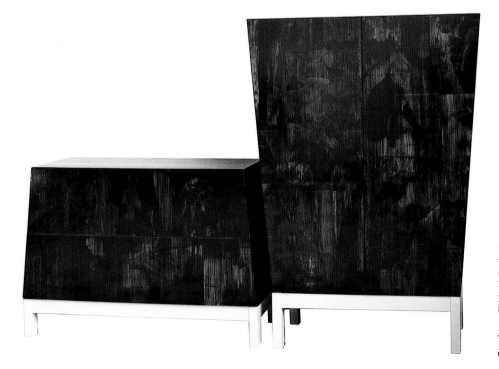

Meaningful themes

A product usually has a tale to tell and this is often steered by an identified theme that provides an element of structure to the design. For example, the Nike Mayfly shoe adopts an insect theme, which is evident in the form and function of the finished product. Themes of this nature can be identified at the beginning of the process or they may evolve during the development of the product as new ideas begin to take shape.

Following a theme helps to suggest boundaries and constraints, and can nudge thinking into particular directions to ensure that there is some consistency throughout a project. However, it does not need to be too literal.

Incorporating a theme can require lateral thinking and can incorporate seemingly tenuous or tangential relationships within the design. Subjectivity, a personal view of beauty and appeal, allows for diversity. This diversity can help products that are different from the norm to instigate debate and become curiously attractive to a range of viewers.

Although an object may appear chaotic or even confused, it can usually retain some order of communication, as the cohesion of individual aspects has been considered by the designer. An appearance of chaos does not mean poor design – quite the reverse. Chaos itself can be a theme and can require a great deal of planning to achieve.

Alternatives and unexpected design approaches grab a viewer's attention and imagination. Art that is shocking or unforeseen can be perversely seductive. It is necessary to challenge convention, have fun and dare to be different; otherwise creativity can stagnate. Remember that mistakes are important and can often facilitate the design process.

The Nike Air Mayfly racing shoe
The Mayfly is a lightweight, delicate shoe that, like the aquatic insect, has a short life expectancy in order to perform a specific task with purpose. A ripstop nylon and phylite construction allows the shoe to be effective for approximately 100km. There are also obvious references to the wing detailing of the insect on the outer surface of the shoe.

Design
Nike

Facial expression
The physical appearance
of a face can
communicate strong
messages and imply
meaning.

Photography
Konstantin Sutyagin
Shutterstock Images LLC

Expression

Everyone knows that a simple facial
expression can communicate an immense
amount of information. Most people
understand such delicate and restrained
non-verbal messages instinctively and they
are a key component of human
communication. This is because the slightest
movement of the mouth or eyes can
significantly alter the meaning of what is being
conveyed and can also communicate different
meanings depending on who is observing. This
is something that every good storyteller knows
and exploits. To communicate effectively they
exploit a range of expressions, gestures,
movements and body language.

The same principles of visual language
apply to product design. Simple, subtle
adjustments in the composition of a product
can create an individual identity and convey
a whole range of information. Just as with
a group of people who know each other well
and can share a joke through discreet smiles
or raised eyebrows, occasionally the
languages that are portrayed by objects
can only be read by those who have
a particular insight and would remain
obscure to an outsider.

The impression that a product projects
may be deliberately arranged to convey
a specific message, to a specific audience;
it may also be orchestrated simply for aesthetic
purposes, allowing individuals
to make personal connections.

Seeing the gap

Tangential *adj*. relating
to or along a tangent

'I look for what needs to be done. After all, that's how the universe designs itself.'
Buckminster Fuller, designer, inventor and author

Avio metal chairs
These images show the distinctive personality of the Avio chairs designed by Alberto Dassasso, Vibrazioni – Art Design. The chairs utilise salvaged metal and are constructed through considered manipulation and welding of the material. The honest language of the chairs incorporates the original colour and finish of the reclaimed metalwork.

Design
Alberto Dassasso, Vibrazioni – Art Design

Photography
Alberto Dassasso

Ethical design

Two apparently identical products can be regarded very differently depending on the story of their construction or development. For example, an egg from a free-range hen and one from a battery hen may look and taste the same to the average consumer. However, if the ethically superior story attached to the free-range hen is communicated effectively, then consumers will often perceive a moral difference between the two products and be willing to pay more in order to support a cause they believe in.

Making positive connections

This same principle can be applied to designed items. Seemingly identical products can have very different backgrounds and if an audience is made aware of the morally preferential story associated with one of the options, then a segment of that audience will be willing to support it. For example, if a manufacturer has a reputation for subjecting their workforce to sweatshop conditions, then they will lose a portion of their potential market. Conversely, if a product is constructed using renewable, ethically sourced materials then this will make it more appealing to a morally aware audience – making it more desirable than an apparently identical item.

The relative expense of handcrafted or ethically sourced products is often overshadowed by the belief that the item is unique or morally and socially desirable. Paying extra to be associated with a particular group, or to support a meaningful cause that cannot be physically appreciated, may seem unorthodox but it is undoubtedly an influential factor for the consumer.

How to...
If an improvement to a familiar commodity has a firm foundation and there is a reasonable argument for adopting the change, then the outcome usually introduces an audience to possibilities that fulfil their subconscious aspirations.

However, it can be helpful to make the improvement visually obvious and appealing. For example, consider the question of free-range eggs. Could the carton be redesigned to make it immediately obvious that the eggs come from happier hens and in this way make the product more appealing to animal-loving consumers?

Seeing the gap

Impact

It can be difficult to persuade an audience to adopt a new version of a familiar product; even if the new version is demonstrably morally or practically superior. To combat this reluctance, it can be beneficial for the new design to be noticeably different to the familiar product. In this way it may be possible to generate awareness of the intrinsic difference between the products and force the audience to question their decisions.

Designers have a responsibility to ensure that the products they propose are an improvement on the status quo. When improvements such as increased environmental sustainability are introduced to a product, it is vital that this information is clearly indicated to the consumer. The message should be placed in context, giving the consumer as much information as possible to enable them to make an informed decision.

Credibility

Any new design, however worthy, must have a degree of social credibility in order to reach its intended audience. There are undoubtedly many products that individual consumers might like to subscribe to but decide not to because of the messages it would send out amongst peers. For example, how many more electric cars would be sold if they had a more desirable design that made them truly trendy?

The design process also requires a moral credibility. During the development of a design, if there are a range of options available, and there only appears to be superficial differences between them, it is important to delve deep and uncover the proposal with real value – the product with credibility.

Important moral and ethical elements need to inform every aspect of design thinking and ensure that product solutions have credibility and conscience. The recognition and acceptance of ethical values and messages can ultimately assist in the success of a product.

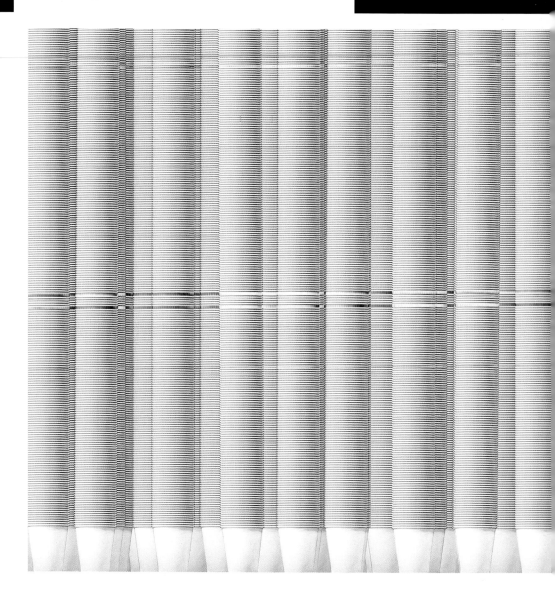

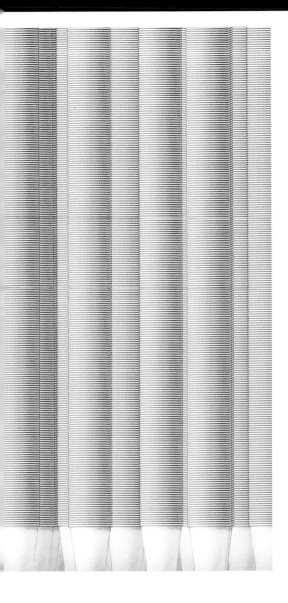

Paper Cups 2008
Paper Cups is taken from
the Running the Numbers
project by Seattle
photographer Chris
Jordan. The project
successfully creates
a better understanding
of impact through the use
of imagery. According
to Chris Jordan, the Paper
Cups 2008 project
'depicts 410,000 paper
cups', a figure that
reflected 'the amount
of throwaway hot-
beverage cups that were
used every 15 minutes
in the United States'.

Designer
Chris Jordan

Shadowing

Our experiences are limited even if we believe that we have encountered much and are culturally well versed. The reason for our restricted understanding is because it has been achieved through a single, biased and often judgemental outlook. We all see the world differently, and simple, innocuous factors can influence the many different ways that everyday tasks are approached.

A fresh perspective

What is good taste and what is considered to be bad taste? Is it quantifiable or simply a subjective opinion? To create a design that will be pleasing, or at least interesting, to a range of tastes it is essential not to be blinkered by our own way of seeing the world. One way to gain a fresh perspective is to shadow a friend or colleague from another discipline for a day. In this way it is possible to experience an unfamiliar philosophy, providing a valuable insight into alternative languages, mannerisms and traits. Looking at and understanding others allows us to understand our own behaviour; to place it into context where it can be more objectively assessed.

How to...
The practice of shadowing is usually conducted through an arrangement that enables an individual to become submerged in an environment that is unfamiliar, or an activity that is perhaps understood but managed by others with a different agenda. The practice can also be conducted by simply entering an unfamiliar environment and trying to interact, or by absorbing an unusual atmosphere.

Shadow *n*. a person secretly following another

Taste *n*. aesthetic discernment

Anthropology *n*. the study of humankind, especially of its societies and customs

Interpretation

The visual languages that constantly surround us are often adapted to accommodate our specific needs and taste. The slight alteration of a visual language in a different environment is like a different dialect, a cultural modification that evolves to serve a particular function more effectively. In order to fully understand the nuances and meaning of an unfamiliar environment it is important to know who to shadow, what to look for and what to observe. However, it is equally important to know how to interpret the unfamiliar visual language that you will encounter. Trying to interpret new and complex visual information can be an arduous task; it is therefore important to discuss findings with the mentor to put what is being learnt into context.

Anthropology

Knowing what to watch and being able to view situations with an open mind is an important aspect of anthropology and as designers we can learn a lot from this branch of social science. Anthropologists are often able to align themselves to the group or individual they are studying; developing a keen understanding of their behaviour and the reasons behind it. It is even common for anthropologists to reach an understanding about the motivations of a particular group of people that goes beyond the group's own understanding. This is because it is very easy to become blind to our own interactions with our environment or the everyday decisions we make that shape our lives. Familiarity and habit mean that we are not the best observers of our own behaviour.

To truly understand how everyday items are used, it is therefore helpful to watch a variety of other people and make a conscious effort to continually question and scrutinise our own behaviour. Watching and understanding contexts requires intuition, an ability to search for clues and indicators and to gather information from an impartial platform. This collection of visual intelligence is assisted through innovative thinking, and the acquisition of physical references. The findings can be further scrutinised at an 'information dump', which is an informal process where objects and findings are openly discussed and reviewed within a group, and where the field work can be placed into context.

Ethical design > **Shadowing** > Mimicry and meaning

 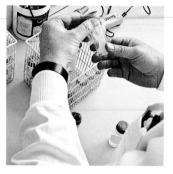 

A photo diary
Shadowing someone
in an unfamiliar
environment can help
us learn new methods
of working and also
understand how other
people use the everyday
items that surround
them. To help remember
and learn more from
the experience it can
be helpful to keep a photo
diary. It is also important
to watch and listen
carefully, without having
a detrimental impact
on the procedures
or activities.

Photography
Tim Harrison

Seeing the gap

How to...
Constraint by our own
self-imposed boundaries
often prevents us from
accepting or looking
towards alternative
cultures. The approved
shadowing of an
individual from another
academic, cultural
or social background
provides an invaluable
guide into the unknown.

Mimicry and meaning

Implied meanings and associations within design are numerous; but things are not always what they appear to be. For example, an object might be designed to deliberately mislead its audience by mimicking a more expensive material or process than has actually been utilised.

Missing the point

Many derivative products that imitate the key features of an innovative design, or which seek to emulate the appearance of a complex production process, often fail to capture the 'soul' of the original item or process. This lack of understanding usually results in an item that is substandard and misplaced, or that is not entirely suitable to its intended purpose.

Despite these difficulties it is still common to attempt to replicate distinctive, desirable attributes across a broad collection of products for a diverse range of reasons. These imitations often miss the hidden complexities and the story that inspired the original item, and it is therefore always worth seriously questioning the impulse to mimic the work of others.

Thematic meaning

Adopting a theme for the development of one's work has the potential to limit as well as inspire. Deciding that a design will have a woodland theme, for example, might place undue limitations on the colours and materials employed if the theme is followed too literally.

However, with sufficient thought and research it is possible to develop a truly insightful understanding of the chosen theme and thereby create designs that are somewhat tangential and more intriguing, enlightening and refreshing as a result. Themes are undoubtedly beneficial to steer one's thinking, and even when a very specific concept has been established, the possibilities and opportunities still remain almost endless.

A great example of this comes from designers Valentina Audrito and Abhishake Kumbhat in their collection Le Uova Di Leon. They demonstrate an innate understanding of the simple form and language of the egg to innovatively and imaginatively create a collection that reflect the primary characteristics without being too prescriptive.

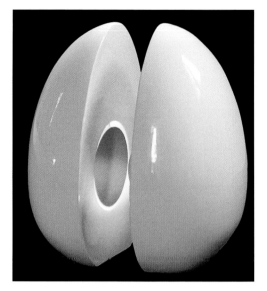

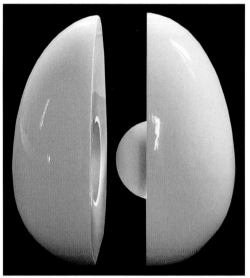

Le Uova Di Leon
The elegant and desirable Le Uova Di Leon collection shows the diverse range of opportunities that were explored and demonstrated using a simple egg theme. The results are both playful and chic.

Designer
Valentina Audrito and Abhishake Kumbhat

Targeted communication

In conversation it is often the tone of voice and body language of the speaker that most effectively communicates their meaning. These aural and visual indicators are often more important, and more quickly understood, than the actual words being spoken.
For example, if a message is urgent (such as 'watch out for that car!') and requires an immediate response from the recipient (such as getting out of the way of danger), then the person speaking is likely to speak and behave in an exaggerated way. They will probably shout and wave at the person in danger. The urgency of the message is communicated through the delivery of the words as much as through the words themselves.

The same is often true with visual languages, for example if a product is dangerous this needs to be made immediately and unavoidably obvious. The same statement can be delivered using a broad array of approaches and with each individual style of delivery the message adopts a slightly different context. For example, a pesticide container might carry the phrase 'harmful if ingested' in small type or it might include a large skull and crossbones. The same message is being communicated but which version of the message would be more immediately effective?

Established languages

Another quick way to communicate an important message is to borrow an already familiar language. For example, we all know that many dangerous insects and plants tend to use bright colours (particularly red or black and yellow stripes) to advertise their capabilities and discourage other animals from tampering with them. These colours therefore encourage a natural caution and reticence, and are often used in the packaging of products that need careful handling.

Toy gun
The language of a real gun is practical and functional, it does not require superfluous ornamentation and decoration; it simply needs to perform its function. Its design is meant to discourage use. In contrast a toy gun, an imitation, adopts a significantly different language when it embraces elements of play not usually allied to the genuine item.

Photography
Clive McCarthy

Seeing the gap

The appearance of a design and the message it portrays to onlookers are fundamental to its initial acceptance by an objective audience. If it is visually unappealing or uninteresting and the information being conveyed is overly complex, uncoordinated or unclear then the intended audience will be turned off – they will not take the trouble to investigate further.

The aesthetic language of an object can be a persuasive, compelling and emotive element. An aesthetically pleasing or interesting design is capable of creating intrigue and can help guide the audience or user to reach a desired conclusion. The arrangement of an object can be deliberately punctuated and orchestrated to tell a story; a story that should flow naturally and avoid any frivolous expression and diversion. A design that is uncomplicated and intuitive demonstrates natural harmony and beauty without being physically constrained.

When aesthetic judgement has not been compromised by clutter and conflict the ensuing message appears simple, pure and accessible. This does not mean that the aesthetics of a product need to be safe or dull. New combinations and experimentation provide significant interest; awakening thinking and assisting in the acceptance and knowledge of a design.

A one flower bouquet
This design explores the language of flowers by constructing a single flower from the elements of various other flowers. This technique manages to communicate a range of messages and has provoked a range of contrasting emotions in its viewers. The surreal outcome may be considered as being both beautiful and ugly.

Design
Todd Bracher, Efe Buluc and Mark Goetz at to22

Unusual approaches

What constitutes or defines a product? Is it the materials, the scale, the production methods, or perhaps the process? A product does not cease to be a product simply because it surpasses a certain scale or because a peculiar approach is employed. Nor does it fail to be a product if an unfamiliar method of production has been used.

Monster designs

Products can be built on an unusual scale, they can use unfamiliar materials and they can go beyond the anticipated – all without disrupting the creative language of the design.

The important question is not what constitutes a product, but rather what mindset is being employed by the designer and what questions they are asking of their audience. The method of thinking, the approach to solving problems or finding plausible and delightful solutions, enables designers to engage with diverse languages. The ability to tell a story is demonstrated through the output of creative maestros such as Philippe Starck who has designed products ranging from pasta to buildings. As designers we must not be afraid to explore different disciplines; to remain creative it is important to be inquisitive and respond to challenges. It is the thinking and imagination that are important, the ability to do something different, tell a unique story and explore interesting languages.

frog: federal republic of germany
Designer Hartmut Esslinger and partners Andreas Haug and Georg Spreng founded Esslinger Design in 1969 using the maxim 'form follows emotion'. The innovative company captured the imagination of German electronics company, WEGA, and produced products including the sculptural WEGA 3020 television in 1970. WEGA were subsequently taken over by Sony, creating an incredible opportunity for the young Esslinger Design studio to work on some of the most prestigious projects of the period.

The distinctive, sculptural aesthetic of Esslinger Design also appealed to Apple, and consequently in 1981, the company adopted the name 'frog design inc.', moved to California, and formed a very productive relationship with them. The vision and capacity to challenge and question directions has helped them become a prominent strategic-creative company creating solutions for Fortune 500 clients. The creative reputation of frog design is global and has seen the company work for clients such as Disney, Microsoft and Yahoo! Frog design has creative, multidisciplinary teams in its studios in the United States, Europe and China and their headquarters are located in San Francisco.

'As long as you are going to be thinking, think big.'

Donald Trump, American entrepreneur

Sony Trinitron
The ability to play with
scale, to see things
differently and not
to categorise is something
that is demonstrated –
by frog design – with
a toy figure football
match on a flat-screen
television. The clarity
of the players echoes
the sophistication of the
cutting-edge technology.

Design
frog design inc

Peeling Project and The Indeterminate Façade Building
An imaginative visual language for the BEST Products Company by the innovative New York architectural group SITE, challenged thinking and asked questions about design. The ability to confront anticipated expectations with unconventional approaches attracted considerable interest.

The Peeling Project Showroom, Richmond, Virginia, 1971, managed to successfully couple art and architecture with its distinctive brick façade.

The Indeterminate Façade Building, Houston, Texas, 1974, challenged aesthetic perceptions with a building that appeared to be in a state of partial degradation.

Design
SITE

**The Tilt Showroom and
The Notch Showroom**
The Tilt Showroom,
Towson, MD, 1978,
demonstrates a language
where an opening
is formed through the
complete structure tilting
backwards.

The Notch Showroom,
Sacramento, CA, 1977,
continued the thinking
with a corner of the
building that appears
to have broken off
to create an opening.

Design
SITE

Alternatives

An alternative solution, which deliberately encourages and seeks out previously untold messages, can provide outcomes that are rewarding and stimulating.

Familiarity breeds contempt and observers can grow accustomed to a particular message and oblivious to any meaning that it is trying to oommunicate. A situation can become tired and passive, but radical changes can introduce a dynamic element, something unforeseen, that forces a design to be categorised differently.

It is not always the case that a preconceived view or a customary fashion for doing something is the most suitable approach. Questions should always be asked and alternative dialogues considered.

Objects are usually created to communicate a specific message or instigate a particular reaction; however, reverse psychology can also be beneficial in getting a necessary message across.

Opposites

Occasionally there are reasons to say something visually that is the opposite of what is meant to ensure that an underlying message is communicated.

The utilisation of opposite terminology can ensure that any anticipated visual bias is challenged:

Functional → Emotional

Conservative → Avant-garde

Ugly → Beautiful

Physical → Spiritual

Robust → Delicate

Complicated → Pure

Mundane → Fun

Threatening → Friendly

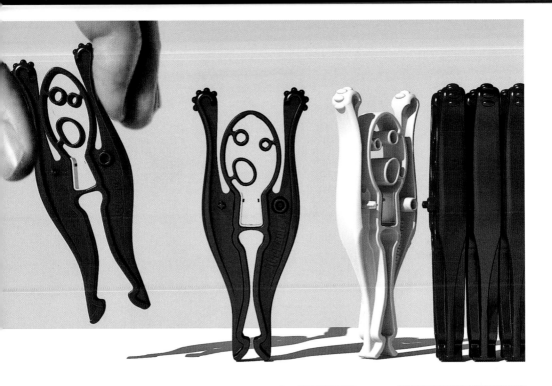

Help!
The Help! character, with its seemingly distressed screaming appearance is a reworking of a mundane wooden peg.

The unexpected language manages to make an emotional and functional connection with the user through aesthetic fun.

Design
Daniele Tomassoni for Biqquadro

How to...
A proposal that needs to prevent a particular situation from occurring should not always set out with a negative mindset.

An approach that assumes a detrimental reaction and responds in an antagonistic manner will invariably aggravate a situation. Something that endorses respect and belief rather than mistrust may well achieve a better reception through the message it sends out.

Substituting conventional messages for opposite statements is frequently beneficial.

Relationships

A product is surrounded and occupied by a myriad of relationships. For example, there is an obvious association between a product and its immediate environment and the space it resides in. An object may merge into its surrounding with minimal disturbance or may be designed to brashly conflict with its environment – to project a loud, seemingly arrogant presence.

The message that a product sends out to the intended user should form a relationship, a bond that is appropriate and easily understood. If a story becomes too sophisticated or too bland, it might not be suitable for the anticipated audience, as it simply fails to engage them.

A product can be deliberately created to be at a level above an individual's literal requirements in order to be better than its competitors or to impress the user. In such cases an advanced, visual language is beneficial in forming a relationship, albeit somewhat superficially.

In circumstances where a theme has been selected a relationship is formed between the object and the source of reference, directing the style of any communication.

A product must also talk with itself, to ensure that individual components sit comfortably and aim to present a unified front. Hierarchy and historical referencing may need to be acknowledged and incorporated in the configuration of an object. A family of products, from a particular background, usually share distinguishing features to reinforce the pedigree and benefit from previous statements associated with the collection.

Minimizing Einstein
The Minimizing Einstein radio challenges conventional thinking and considers how a product might be constructed if functional elements, such as switches and dials were removed and an understanding between shape and material was physically expressed.

The relationship between volume and speaker is echoed through the scale, with larger components representing increased sound. Similarly, physical movements of the antenna would be required for channel adjustments.

Design
Demakersvan

Talking aesthetically

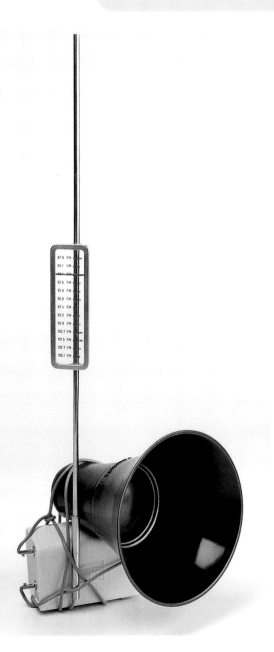

'We are storytellers, from fantasy to factory, from statement to product.'

Demakersvan

Demakersvan
Dutch designers Jeroen Verhoeven, Joep Verhoeven and Judith de Graauw form the design group Demakersvan, 'the makers of'.
The team met at the renowned Design Academy in Eindhoven and have created designs such as 'Lace Fence', 'Lost & Found Stool' and the stunning 'Cinderella table'.

The Minimizing Einstein radio designed by Judith de Graauw reflects the group's approach to creating conceptual and engaging pieces that challenge design thinking, like much of the inspirational work found in contemporary Dutch design.

Demakersvan have worked with many of the world's leading designers, and the work of the group has been exhibited in influential galleries such as the Victoria & Albert Museum, London, and the Museum of Modern Art (MOMA), New York.

Art and industry

The beautiful and elegant Taccia lamp designed by Achille and Pier Giacomo Castiglioni in 1958, produced by FLOS from 1962, embraces sculptural aesthetics with acute industrial awareness. The uncomplicated and practical relationship between art and industry captured within the sophisticated lamp was the designers' creative response to exploring simple lighting and materials.

The Taccia lamp has a fluted, extruded aluminium cylinder that shrouds the bulb and consequently radiates heat away. An adjustable, hand-blown parabolic glass curve confidently rests upon the cylinder to support a graceful reflector that bounces light out. The practical and unrestricted assembly of these core industrial components manages to reinforce an overall statement of simplicity and conceals the complex investigation and creative astuteness of the designers.

The juxtaposition of industry and sculpture is demonstrated in the numerous innovative products conceived from the practical approach and enquiry of Achille and Pier Giacomo Castiglioni, including the 1962 Toio floor lamp and the impressive Arco floor lamp for FLOS.

Taccia lamp
The Taccia floor lamp designed by Achille and Pier Giacomo Castiglioni in 1958 and manufactured by FLOS from 1962.

Design
Achille and Pier Giacomo Castiglioni, FLOS

Photography
Piero Fasanotto

Talking aesthetically

Christy Sugar Bowl
The charming Christy
Sugar Bowl (1993)
produced by Alessi,
is a descendant of
a silver-plated design
created more than
a century before by the
prestigious artist,
craftsman and designer
Christopher Dresser
for Elkington & Co in
Birmingham, England.
The Christy Sugar Bowl
design by Alessi is
credited to Christopher
Dresser (1864).

Design
Alessi Spa,
Crusinallo, Italy.

Unusual approaches > Skins

Skins

The skin of a product assumes a range of significant functions and responsibilities. The predominant tasks being to conceal, protect and articulate.

External

The external façade of a product is usually crafted in order to perform a range of primary and secondary functions. Practical elements that embrace the maxim 'form follows function' are considered carefully as the outward-looking face of an object is often the predominant communicating tool that needs to attract, inform and suggest. The external surface is not simply a shape without additional purpose, but rather a defined and considered structure that should imply and direct the language of an object. The outer skin is seldom a bland structure but a diverse, complex and suggestive surface that exudes meaning. The external surface offers the opportunity to present and expose individual messages to ultimately create a unified statement.

The language communicated by an external surface can also be enhanced or reduced depending on its immediate surroundings. A design developed without consideration to a surrounding context may ultimately fail. The immediate space around a product can be controlled to a point through careful design and by developing an empathy with how users might interact with the product. The abstract space surrounding an object can also inform the development of products and inspire alternative thinking and languages.

The inspirational design group to22 recognised the importance of abstract space in the development of their Second Skin bowl for Industreal. The negative space that was observed surrounding objects became the creative stimulus, a third-party language that dictated the overall form in the generation of Second Skin.

'We want to create a container, which is not designed. Its expression comes from the objects it holds. Fruit is clustered together. The object is the material which surrounds it.'

to22, designers

Second Skin

The approach of to22 is to look and consider things in a different context and to employ alternative thinking. Second Skin is a beautiful object that has been realised by appreciating the space that envelops objects rather than simply creating an object.
The beauty of Second Skin is undoubtedly the ability to think laterally and differently.

Design

Todd Bracher, Efe Buluc and Mark Goetz (to22) for Industreal®. All rights reserved.

Photography

Ilvio Gallo

Unusual approaches > **Skins** > Disguise

'The language of products is a language that we give them
so that they can communicate with users.'

Jurgen Bey, Bright Ideas, Beautiful Minds

Internal

The internal surface of a product might
be considered to have a less dominant
communication role compared to the outer
skin unless it is periodically exposed, the
surfaces merge or it is continually visible due
to its inherent make-up. Although the internal
face may often be hidden from view to an
end user, the inner sanctum undoubtedly
has the capacity to communicate a broad
range of messages.

An internal surface can communicate
messages through touch rather than visually
present information. Tactile awareness
is particularly sensitive and can often reveal
information and detail, which might not
be understood or accessed through
observation alone. The sculptural statements
of artists such as Henry Moore (1898–1986)
and works such as Two Large Forms are
undoubtedly enhanced and better understood
through touch complementing the visual.

The inner surface of an object is often
the location for hidden detail, the scars
of production which are not expected to
be read, but can be sought out and provide
an indication of how an object emerged.

**Kokon Furniture:
Table-chair**
Disused, abandoned and
forgotten pieces of
furniture are transformed
and afforded distinctive
identities when coupled
together with a synthetic
skin. The fluidity of the
skin masks the previous
character of the furniture
and reveals a unique,
sculptural language. In
addition to the Table-chair
the experimentation also
included Chair & child's
chair, Double-chair,
Wall-chair and Long-chair.

Design
Jurgen Bey for Droog

Photography
Marsel Loermans

Talking aesthetically

Confronting difficulties

If a design element feels wrong then
it probably is wrong and it may be worthwhile
beginning to seek alternative solutions.
A designer's intuition, how they feel about
particular elements of their work, can lead
them to identify anomalies with the aesthetic
appearance of an object. However, there
is a fundamental difference between feeling
and knowing what is wrong. It is often the
case that a small adaptation or reinterpretation
might be sufficient to fix the problem.
Unfortunately, there is rarely a quick-fix
solution when a design simply isn't working.
When we begin to make small adjustments
to one aspect of a design it can cause or bring
to light other areas of concern. Confronting
a seemingly small problem with one aspect
of a design can instigate an entire rethink
of the overall visual message of the product.

It is common for a design to seem
too ordinary or too familiar. It is very easy
to become accustomed to a single way
of thinking about a particular product, which
can lead to lazy habits and mental short
cuts to produce dull and uninspired designs.
Innovation and alternatives can challenge
the familiar and present exciting opportunities.
If ideas and innovations are not allowed
to surface, then the monotony of the usual
will prevail and the result is unlikely to please
either the designer or the intended audience.

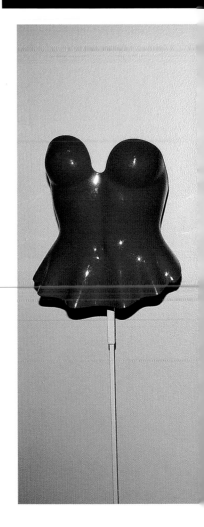

Love and War: The Weaponized Woman

The Love and War: The Weaponized Woman exhibition at the prestigious Fashion Institute of Technology in New York featured designs in 2006 by premier fashion designers accustomed to challenging conventions and who understood the importance of cross-disciplinary references.

Issey Miyake created the beautiful and alluring red fibreglass bodice; the Yohji Yamamoto corset combined wood, metal and felt, whilst Hussein Chalayan also expressed the beauty of fibreglass with the construction of the statuesque and gracefully contoured dress.

Design
Issey Miyake, Yohji Yamamoto and Hussein Chalayan

Photography
Robyn Beck/AFP/ Getty Images

Unusual approaches > **Skins** > Disguise

Organic

Necessity can be a persuasive and compelling force in determining the structure and aesthetic language of an object. 'Need' rarely accommodates beautification but ironically when form follows function, with stringent and controlled approaches, a beautifully pure object may emerge. An organic form is a form that has evolved and developed through requirement, a sensitive and accommodating morphology that is typically an incremental improvement on previous solutions.

Nature manages to carefully refine and perfect embryonic forms to become pared, sophisticated languages with a fluidity that is elegant and economical. The approach is echoed in products that assume an organic narrative. A simple façade that can consume or erase visual irregularities can transform a complicated arrangement into an unflustered and sculptural object.

A simple skin that engulfs the disparate elements of a product and consequently obscures any distinguishing definition can also appear unfamiliar and alien. An object that is emotionally appealing but has no defined characteristics relies on sensory features, such as tactility and intuitive interaction, to successfully communicate primary messages.

How to...
Identifying an awkward aesthetic language, a creative blemish that is visually uncomfortable, is not something that can always be understood immediately although it may generate an uneasy reaction.

It is not always a straightforward activity to research difficulties in aesthetic languages as it is often the case that an initial relationship between user and object needs to be determined. The observation and recording of difficult aesthetic languages are something that should be documented as and when they present themselves or when something manages to disturb.

FROG camera – '5 Systems' model
The unique biomorphic compact underwater camera FROG was part of the '5 Systems' proposal submitted by Luigi Colani as part of a design research project in 1983. The proposed designs, as embodied in the models shown here, were based on the cutting-edge technology Canon expected to have available by the 1990s. The proposed camera was envisioned as being capable of capturing 150 frames to enable sustained periods of underwater photography.

Design
Luigi Colani for Canon Inc.
Courtesy of Canon Inc.

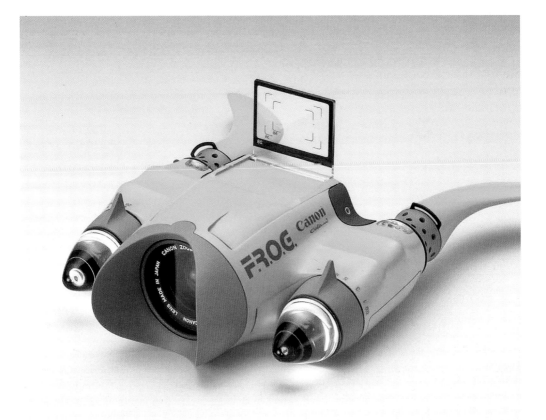

Luigi Colani (b. 1928)

German designer Luigi Colani is a prophet of form, an undisputed design visionary who studied sculpture, painting and aerodynamics, and undoubtedly, like many designers and architects, identifies Mother Nature as a design mentor. A diverse and stimulating designer, Professor Luigi Colani's work instantly captures the imagination with a language that evokes organic references and manages to successfully merge the seemingly juxtaposed elements of reality and fantasy.

There appears to be no limitation to the challenges that the Colani Studios are able to undertake and subsequently develop. The ability to nudge contemporary thinking in innovative and exciting directions has ensured that Professor Luigi Colani has remained at the forefront of design for over five decades.

Hy-Pro and Super C.Bio – '5 Systems' models

The sculpted structure of the Canon Hy-Pro, with its harmonious and beautifully tactile language, encourages interaction and reflects the living forms that inspired its creation. The smooth, muted narrative is a consequence of sensitivity and need. The Hy-Pro was designed to be used in various modes to accommodate user requirements.

The Super C.Bio SLR camera was inspired by the T70 camera and adopted a complex and organic user-friendly fluid form.

Design

Luigi Colani for Canon Inc.
Courtesy of Canon Inc.

**Lady and HOMIC –
'5 Systems' models**
The Lady was envisioned
as a simple-to-operate
camera and attention
was particularly applied
to how the sculpted
product could be
comfortable to operate.
The overall language
perception of Colani's
1983 camera concept is
simplicity, which is
reinforced through the
clean lines and purity of
the appearance.

The Horizontal
Memorychip Integral
storobo Camera (HOMIC)
is perhaps the most
unusual of the '5 systems'
collection. The HOMIC
was designed as a still
video camera encased in
a form reminiscent of
a variety of living forms.
The unusual form and
language that the camera
design adopted to
perform the required
function also ensured that
it would capture the
attention of others.

Design
Luigi Colani for Canon Inc.
Courtesy of Canon Inc.

Disguise

The language of a product can be disguised or hidden through a lack of information and clarity. When a designer's primary objective is to create a pure, uncluttered aesthetic, there is a danger that the outcome may be bland or uninteresting.

Minimalism and clutter

The aesthetic of minimalism, the desire to retain a pure simple design, should be treated with caution when it begins to override the needs of the design. If the aesthetic form of the design is given precedence over its primary function then the results can be disastrous. Innumerable products are concealed within a bland and sterile covering, which conceals the workings and often the function of the design. The intended audience can't see how the product works or what it is meant to do and therefore it fails to engage their attention.

On the other hand, it is possible to go too far the other way. Many designers react to the multitude of featureless and nondescript products by embracing a multitude of languages and references. In contrast to a basic or simple mentality that concentrates on purity, a busy and cluttered object can also prevent a message from surfacing. A product that has no management and no control over language can become confused when eclectic styles create visual 'chatter' that conceals the purpose of the design. Embellishment and ornamentation lose sight of the fundamental messages and can impede underlying messages just as much as over-simplification.

Memphis

Design group Memphis, founded in 1981, created a myriad of highly creative and visually stimulating objects and textiles such as the Super Lamp designed by Martine Bedin (1981) and D'Antibes cabinet designed by George Sowden (1981). The forward-looking and inspirational dialogues that were pursued by the Memphis members were a significant contrast to the bland and lacklustre products that were becoming prevalent at the time.

Minimalism *n.*
a movement in sculpture and painting which arose in the 1950s, characterised by the use of simple, massive forms

Fashion and evolution

Fashions change for many reasons and they affect everything from the clothes that we wear to the attitudes we hold and the everyday products and environments that we live with. The visual language of objects can become dated when more fashionable thinking patterns emerge and directions are amended to become aligned with popular culture and trends.

Change is stimulating and natural; it alleviates the monotony of being subjected to the same messages and stories. A product that captures the culture of the moment and embraces tangential thinking retains user interest and can be vibrant and exciting.

Most contemporary products have a shifting audience with ever more demanding expectations. For example, user expectations for telephones have changed beyond recognition in recent years. Constant technological innovations in this category mean that designers must now anticipate improvements and reflect them in the language of their designs.

With fast-changing products such as this, the metamorphosis of its design may be forced and hastily conducted – with design solutions being required quickly due to circumstances outside the designer's control.

Another reason for a product's design changing quickly is economic difficulty – where limited funding and resources dictate the production methods and materials used. Although design thinking should not be fundamentally impaired whatever the circumstance, what is actually achievable during an economic downturn or depression can be impressive. Innovative practices need to be taken up that can respond to any imposed constraint to ensure that viable outcomes are achievable. Design is primarily about common sense and creativity, and being able to learn from previous mistakes. An enforced constraint of any description is a challenge, not a barrier, and something that should be overcome.

Characteristics

Why are some products destined to become characterless objects with no soul? Many products are faceless companions, objects that a user interacts with every day but does not feel an attachment to because they have no interesting features.

It can all be interesting

It can appear that some everyday objects are destined always to be average, but all objects should be designed carefully irrespective of any other criteria. There is no hierarchy to creative attention. Commonplace objects from toothbrushes to toilet brushes are not exempt from character and inspirational designers such as Michael Graves and Philippe Starck have embraced the ordinary to set new creative precedents.

Objects that conform to mediocrity are uninspiring and dull as nothing original is offered and they do not vie for the user's attention. Lifeless is meaningless.

Give it character

Every product should have an inherent character and be given care and attention in its configuration. A product might be good, or it might be sublime; it is character that makes the difference. A simple, carefully considered modification or an elementary makeover such as an adjustment to a fundamental line or the slight movement of a feature in the arrangement of a product, can drastically transform the item from something that is perceived as bland, to something that is engaging and appealing.

A basic alteration to meaning, the amendment of semantic messages, can instantly generate a constructive feeling rather than portray a disparaging or ordinary sentiment.

Waiting Chairs

A waiting room chair does not need to be boring or to suggest that the ensuing encounter is going to be dreary. A chair, with a bit of thought to its semantics, could be created to generate a smile and promote relaxation.

With the Waiting Chairs, Demakersvan use chairs to portray the body language of individuals waiting.

Design
Demakersvan

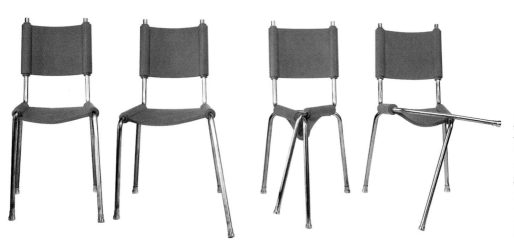

Zoomorphic design

The appeal of an object can be enhanced through an association or partial implementation of an animal characteristic or attribute. References that are made may be comprehensive or of a cosmetic nature and tend to be articulated in a lateral capacity rather than expressed in a literal sense, as accurate translations are often tortuous. The purpose of suggesting a correlation between object and animal is to complement or reaffirm a particular aspect of a story that may also support the design's overall message.

An advantage of referencing subtle animal traits is that they are usually instinctively understood by the audience and can therefore prompt them to make appropriate connections between the design and the animal. A reference can originate from a simple microbe or a complex animal; it is the way that the information is interpreted that is significant.

How to…
Desirable and distinctive animal qualities that are reflected in the aesthetic make-up of an object are often exaggerated to stress a relationship. Adjectives that are allied to features in the natural world can be transposed to the physical world through careful evaluation and interpretation.

Imagine an object and consider what the item might be if it were an animal. Contemplate the core messages that need to be communicated and how a lateral association between creature and object may be formed. The transition of information does not need to be a holistic reflection, but rather a selected feature or attribute that is central to the story to be told.

Lucellino and Birds Birds Birds
Lucellino captures the delicate, fragile nature of a small bird through the use of little more than a bulb and handcrafted goose-feather wings. The apparent simplicity of the design with feathers attached directly to the bulb to form a pair of wings was balanced with touch-tronic sophistication that echoed the sensitivity of a small bird.

In contrast to the imagery of the Lucellino, the Birds Birds Birds chandelier reflected the sight of a group of birds taking flight. Magnificent 24 low-voltage bulbs, with individual goose-feather wings, were perched on wires that could be manipulated by the user to create their own unique arrangement.

Design
Ingo Maurer

Photography
Tom Vack

Talking aesthetically

**Birdie and
Birdie's Nest**
Birdie, a smaller
chandelier than
the previous Birds Birds
Birds design, invited
the user to compose
an arrangement of 12
low-voltage bulbs, again
perched on individual
wires, in any direction,
in order to create the
chaotic explosion of birds
in flight.

Birdie's Nest is comprised
of ten low-voltage bulbs.

Design
Ingo Maurer

Photography
Tom Vack

Ingo Maurer (b. 1932)
German lighting designer
Ingo Maurer initially
trained as a graphic
designer in Germany
and Switzerland before
practising as a freelance
designer in the United
States in the period
1960–1963. Ingo Maurer
returned to Europe and
started Design M in 1966.

The incredible
designs of Ingo Maurer,
such as Porca Miseria!,
Blushing Zettel'z and
the prototype Oh Man,
it's a Ray demonstrate
the fantastic array
of materials that are
used to merge beauty
and functionality in the
manipulation of light.

Porca Miseria! used
porcelain, Blushing
Zettel'z utilised Japanese
paper, and Oh Man
it's a Ray utilised coat
hangers – a reference
to the 1920 work
Obstruction by the
American Dadaist and
Surrealist photographer
and artist, Man Ray.

Disguise > Characteristics

Enjoyment

The language of products designed
for a younger generation often manages
to embrace the characteristics of fun and play.
The 'My First Sony' range developed during
the 1980s included a headset walkie-talkie,
radio cassette player and radio cassette-
corder, as well as a 'Walkman' and other
products aimed at capturing the imagination
of children. The collection carefully addressed
visual language issues and used a combination
of robust aesthetics and primary colours
that the user could instinctively understand.
The use of friendly icons replaced conventional
and perhaps more sophisticated instructions
and again ensured that the experience could
be enjoyed.

In addition, Sony also managed to colour
code the various functions of the products
in the range, making it much easier to interact
with additional 'My First Sony' products.

An empathy with language, fun and
the user is more recently demonstrated
with the delightful range of products created
by frog design and Disney, in which visual
messages unite to formulate an attractive
and exciting outcome.

Talking aesthetically

Disney Consumer Electronics

Disney approached frog design to create a range of consumer electronics that embraced the Disney brand in 2003. A fun two-way radio and cordless phone, which successfully utilised Motorola technology, echoed the exciting language of Disney. Further products including TV, DVD and CD player, were subsequently produced with similar control and sensitivity.

Design

frog design inc

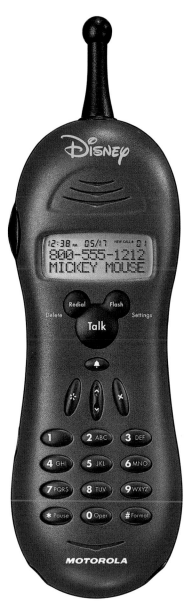

Disguise > **Characteristics**

Before we can truly understand the requirements of a design and its audience we must first observe the ways in which they interact. If possible, these observations should take place in a real-life, natural context. When information is gathered in a contrived environment many important details can be missed.

By observing the way that users interact with their surroundings we can identify the small but important details that can make everyday objects that little bit more interesting and engaging.

Not all of these details have to have a serious purpose. Surprises and unexpected details can reflect subtle observations and connect directly with the audience. The development of interesting and engaging designs does not require an ambitious or elaborate framework; it simply requires a realistic vision and a little common sense.

When working on a new design it is important to think carefully about what is needed, how it might be attained and when to stop. It is usually best to keep things simple; even when the development of a design has been complex, the outcome should appear as natural as possible. Simple design is good design – but it can also be fun.

Caterpillar Stool/Bench
This creatively simple, interlocking design allows the form to become whatever a child's imagination wants it to be. In this case it is creative thinking rather than ambiguous detail that directs understanding.

Design
Alberto Marcos for ninetonine

Talking aesthetically > **Taming the thought** > Performing

Targeting you!

A personal connection between product and user is often needed if the item is to be fully understood. Individuals, each with their own specific expectations and demands, are steadily replacing the collective target market and designers must respond accordingly. Markets are made up of individuals each with their own identity and experiences; markets are not made up of stereotypes.

Getting focused

Individual consumers want products to suit their specific needs – not the predicted needs of their demographic group. To achieve this many users now expect to be able to manipulate and shape the products they buy so that they perfectly suit their requirements. However, these same consumers still expect mass production efficiency and are not willing to pay a one-off premium price.

Products need to connect and engage the individual, instil a feeling of confidence and importance rather than be a random and impersonal object where communication strategies are left to chance with 'a one-size-fits-all' approach.

Private conversations, the one-to-one talks between an individual and an object, are undeniably more desirable than being part of a crowd where one statement and one solution are delivered to everyone indiscriminately.

Products do need to be flexible. They need to embrace dialects and merge desire with need by recognising that every conversation and every person is unique. The consumer can no longer be treated as a faceless statistic. They now need to be perceived as individuals – real people, with real lives and high expectations of the products they purchase.

Cultural identification

Fashions can change quickly, and neither following them nor trying to anticipate them guarantees success. However, observing the habits and behaviour of a target audience can provide invaluable ideas for developing new products to suit the needs of that group. These ideas can then be further developed in order to push the culture forward – rather than simply mimicking what already exists.

An idea cannot simply be regurgitated into another product and expected to succeed. Successful contribution to an existing cultural aesthetic requires much more than a literal translation of what already exists.

Similarly, the multiple identities of an individual (such as their work lives, home lives and social lives) often mean that a product is acceptable for someone in a certain climate but is entirely unacceptable in an alternative context. It is therefore very difficult to accurately assess everything that an individual requires from a product from seeing them in a single context. Individuals present things differently depending on their surroundings and the same is evident with products. Observation and adaptation of a culture is helpful, but remember that it is also fun to be different and take a chance on something new.

YPPY® Walkman collection

In Autumn/Winter '95 and Spring/Summer '96 Sony released the distinctive and rare YPPY® Walkmans. The designs adopted a street language that was undeniably unique and reflected different genres of musical taste. The collection managed to combine elements of fun, fashion and originality.

Sony and Walkman are trademarks of the Sony Corporation, Japan.

Design
Sony

Adaptations

Everybody is different and we all have our own mannerisms, desires and features that distinguish us from everybody else. Faces are different, clothes are different, experiences are different and languages are different. There are numerous individual factors that contribute to the overall make-up of an individual that ensures that everyone remains unique and interesting. The components that make us so individual are not static but are constantly changing, evolving and developing as individuals re-invent themselves. A design that fails to take into account that everyone is individual and that everybody has a fluctuating character will be less useful than a product that can evolve, adapt and echo the changes of its audience.

The evolution of design relies on designers with an ability to recognise change and react accordingly; a case of 'survival of the most aware'. Products that are composed from simple and effective components can be readily configured to make an array of statements that can be fashioned to directly liaise with the user. A product that is able to re-invent itself can become what the user would like it to be. A product should function correctly and have the capacity to respond and create a feel-good factor.

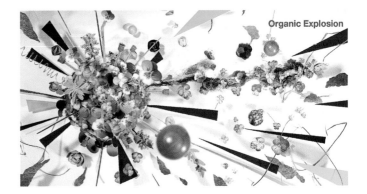

Organic Explosion

**Organic Explosion,
Green and More,
Swatch Sepaflor**
The florally adorned
Swatch Spring/Summer
2009 Organic Explosion
Collection builds on the
diversity of the Swatch
range and is centred
on simple and effective
quality.

Design
Swatch Ltd

Swatch
The Swatch was
developed in response
to the increasing
competition, particularly
from Japan, faced by
the Swiss watch industry
in the mid 1970s.
The arrival of the
Swatch in 1983 signified
a development that
combined an adaptable
visual language with
affordability – as a result
of using significantly
fewer components
than earlier watches
(51 components, instead
of the usual 91 parts
or more).
    The continued
vision of Swatch and
its ability to respond
effectively to the
demands of a new
generation has seen
it become a recognised
leader in global watch
design.

Targeting you! > Irrational thinking

Irrational thinking

If everyone thought, behaved and felt the same the world would be a very dull place. There would be no debate, no interesting characters, no excitement and no sharing of experiences. There would also be no arguments or disputes to trigger different factions that could compete and explore alternative pathways and languages.

Causing controversy

If everyone was the same then the status quo would never be challenged and life would become increasingly staid and predictable. Controversial ideas can create dialogue and interest within a community; they can have an infectious dynamism that provokes others to new, more inventive work.

An irrational message is a narrative that defies conventions, ignores logic and which may be considered foolish or even absurd. The irrational statement is a live thought; an exciting notion that shouts in the face of all expectations and often seeks a reaction. This approach is particularly adept at changing thinking patterns and causing a pause for thought.

But something irrational is perhaps only categorised as being irrational because it has not previously been considered and deviates from accepted practice; it is a foreign language that is difficult to understand and is often unfairly dismissed for this reason. An attention-seeking statement might be part of an object that still manages to conform and adhere to broadly accepted values and protocols in other ways.

Erwin Wurm (b. 1954)
Austrian artist and sculptor Erwin Wurm avoids excessive complication to ensure that the messages and statements he makes are accessible and immediate.

The 'One Minute Sculpture' series, shown overleaf, which sees individuals in unfamiliar and often surreal circumstances, captures the imagination in a similar fashion to more substantial projects such as the Fat Car (2005) and Fat House (2003), which are a commentary on society.

Contrasting elements are often evident within his work, even when dealing with serious and complex issues. However the messages are not trivial or without depth. Complicated thoughts and meanings are effectively transformed to become simple messages that can be readily understood by a wide audience.

Renault 25 – 1991
Artist Erwin Wurm has
an innate capacity to
question and view simple
things another way.
  He incorporates slight
modifications to what
is expected or presumed
to be normal and although
the changes are small
the impact is considerable
when visual languages
are challenged.

Design
Erwin Wurm

One Minute Sculptures
Simple, diverse,
surprising and engaging,
the One Minute Sculpture
series by artist Erwin
Wurm presents the
unexpected and
the abstract. Messages
are communicated
and situations created
where observers
and participants are
suddenly placed in an
unfamiliar context.

The impact of these
challenging, yet
ephemeral performances
is substantial.

Erwin Wurm
manages to succinctly
demonstrate the power
of communication
and the significance
of a statement.

Design
Erwin Wurm

Unexpected

Just because something has not been
done before does not mean that it should
not be done.

Creativity is about exploring, being intrepid
and challenging convention, although many
products often remain dormant, afraid to talk
and venture into the unknown. Everything
is unfamiliar until it is discovered. The products
that break ranks and explore different
languages and dialogues are often promptly
followed by the masses, until another product
surges forward to push the boundaries
and innovate even further. There are numerous
products that have remained inactive for too
long, unprepared to digress slightly and make
minor modifications to how they are created
and used. Simple design changes can
generate renewed interest from consumers,
who may in turn move the concept forward
through unexpected developments.

Changing Cupboard
This design is part
of Front's FOUND
collection, which
focused on the simple
characteristics
of everyday products.
Changing Cupboard
constantly re-invents
itself and transforms
through the use of
rotating advertising
panels in the façade.
The correlation between
existing objects and
the emerging object was
an underlying theme
within the collection.

Design
Front

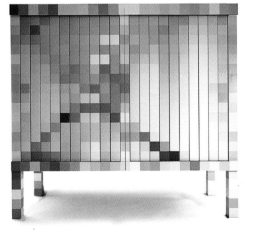

Surprise

A free uninhibited mentality that can combine
eclectic references with assorted visual
languages can conjure up surprises that
tease and taunt the observer. An object
can be manipulated to deliberately defy logic
and belief and as a consequence demands
attention and breeds curiosity. A continual
bombardment of visual messages ensures
that individuals become receptive to the many
different ways that something can be read,
but when a message confronts expectations
it may be bemusing or unsettling and it is not
always obvious why.

A free agenda and the desire to have
fun provide the basis for juggling languages
and experimentation.

Do not believe everything you see. Objects
are frequently constructed to simply astonish
and delight.

**Balancing, Vanishing
and Divided**
The Magic Collection
created by Front
includes Divided –
a gravity-defying chest
of drawers; Vanishing,
a side unit that
disappears; and the
incredible Balancing
chair. The collection,
which also included
Levitating –
a standard lamp that
appears to levitate,
was created following
a productive collaboration
with magicians to
understand and
incorporate their craft.

Design
Front

Irrational *adj*. not logical or reasonable

Expressing fun

Fun has several meanings depending on circumstance and the relationship to a particular experience. A fun feeling might be considered to be a unique emotional experience and although the response or reaction of others may be similar, different characters in different contexts will probably demonstrate a different interpretation.

Getting a reaction

An object can communicate and unite a range of different sensations associated with fun. A sense of joy and happiness can be generated by an object if it is able to fulfil or exceed certain expectations. Joy might be communicated through a number of distinctive visual characteristics, but it might also be communicated through a mental association or memory.

Anticipation and hope may also create a feeling of excitement that can be reinforced by clear and explicit sensory triggers that are instantly recognised by the audience. Fun does not need to mean an obvious outward expression of emotion and can be something pure and restrained that might engender similar feelings in the observer.

Personification

Products that have a direct and intimate contact with the user often have to echo the messages that the individual projects to the world. The product must in some way personify the user. Items such as eyewear function as a fundamental reflection of character. These are highly sensitive items and even seemingly small alterations to their design can have a considerable influence on how the user feels and is perceived.

When a product is a focus of attention and is critically and constantly interrogated by the user and their contacts, every physical and aesthetic element needs careful consideration to ensure the message is unified and comprehensive.

How to...
The broad meaning of fun can be explored through recording feelings in a diary.
Simple notes that refer to everyday experiences will highlight the diversity.

Taming the thought

Alain Mikli eyewear

The acclaimed eyewear by designer Alain Mikli explores in detail the function and language of design to set a creative standard. A sophisticated and controlled awareness of contemporary thinking and style, which is not restricted to mundane attitudes and repetitive scenarios, ensures that Alain Mikli eyewear exudes personality.

Designers including Issey Miyake, Alyson Magee and Sara Eliris have developed eyewear collections that are distinctive, sensitive and beautiful.

Design
Alain Mikli

Personify *v.*
attribute a personal nature or human characteristics to something non-human

Irrational thinking > **Expressing fun** > Interactive play

Interactive play

Interactive designs that encourage their audience to play with them often leave users feeling that the designers have genuinely taken their feelings into account. Messages that are formulated using stimulating and imaginative approaches may appear to be more personal than generic, and are consequently more adept at attracting the attention of their audience.

Feeling special

The reality is that the emotions experienced by users interacting with a product are often encountered by many recipients and that the communication is often more public than private. The ability to engage, transfix and entertain is an underlying characteristic of interactive play that is perhaps not evident in more conventional scenarios.

An artefact that communicates a distinct message to a passive or interested observer usually manages to be noticed simply because it rouses the senses and is difficult to ignore.

A message that is conveyed directly to an individual or in the immediate vicinity of a passer-by can form a relationship that is an impulsive, temporary connection. Interactive play has the ability to put users at ease and to help them enjoy time out. An individual who has been lured by the unfamiliar is often keen to know more but the complete or anticipated message is not always forthcoming and simply stimulates curiosity. Despite the communication strategy having a broad appeal a definite sense of belonging can transpire.

Cherry Blossom
Cherry Blossom was
an interactive installation
at the Design Triennial,
Cooper-Hewitt, National
Design Museum in 2003
and was located in the
centre of the grand
staircase. Individuals
going up and down the
stairs became interactive
performers when their
movements triggered
swirling blossom.
The steps that were
taken were monitored
through surveillance
cameras, which instigated
the display.
  The movement and
sound of the installation
was directly influenced
by the individuals on the
staircase creating an
exciting and exhilarating
experience. The designers
emphasised the
significance of the users
by ensuring that the
imagery transformed into
snow when there was
no interaction.

Design
Masamichi Udagawa
and Sigi Moeslinger
of Antenna Design
New York Inc.

Photography
Ryuzo Masunaga

Expressing fun > **Interactive play**

Installation

Installations present the opportunity
for individuals to relate directly to objects and
for objects to directly respond in an exciting
and often positive way. Interactive installations
can accommodate multiple users and portray
an array of messages that often appear to be
personal communications.

Any unique encounter that can entertain
the senses is undoubtedly a memorable
experience and something that almost
inadvertently creates intrigue. An installation
is essentially a demonstration of high creativity,
and in many ways an opportunity to explore
alternative languages, experiment and
communicate through fusing media.
The intelligence that is demonstrated in an
interactive installation is invariably an outcome
of freedom of thought and reflective of
a catwalk scenario where inspirational and
creative ideas can influence others.

Thinking and meanings attached to original
installations in the public domain can be
transposed to smaller items in much the same
way as very simple ideas can emerge as
impressive fun statements.

Power Flower

The captivating and enthralling interactive public installation Power Flower developed an ephemeral language for Bloomingdale's New York, Häagen-Dazs Cultural Initiative, 2002. It used a series of iconic neon 'blooms' and sounds that were triggered by people walking past. The ephemeral blooms subsequently diminished in sequence as passers-by moved on, until another interaction occurred.

Design
Masamichi Udagawa & Sigi Moeslinger of Antenna Design New York Inc.

Photography
Ryuzo Masunaga

A presentation is in essence a performance; a piece of theatre where there is an opportunity to take the stage and captivate an audience. The performer, or storyteller, needs to be prepared so that necessary information is communicated in a succinct and professional manner that is appropriate to the situation. However, the performance also needs to ensure that there is opportunity for manoeuvrability and interaction. Meticulous rehearsals can hinder the natural fluidity of a presentation, or show. The groundwork for a performance should be carefully considered so that the pitch of the 'act' is suitably positioned for the intended spectators. Misinformation, surplus or excessive information that does not support the core story should be eradicated from the performance as it can invite digression and confusion.

The purpose of a presentation is to encourage prompt debate and ideally gain support. Audiences are critical, but it is the individual performer that should be the primary critic and ensure that the message being told is suitably entertaining.

Information tent
This tent offers headphones and a comfortable environment as an interactive means to present information to an audience. This kind of advance preparation can enable a presentation to take place without the presence of a presenter.

Photography
Clive McCarthy

Theatre

The theatre is a place of imagination and stories, a place of transitions and where character changes are constantly anticipated. It is an exciting venue for communicating and exchanging ideas with strangers. A performance does not need to be overdressed or complicated; it just needs to be sensitive to requirements.

Rehearsal

First impressions count and it is necessary to recognise that different circumstances require different approaches when formulating a presentation strategy. Understanding the background to a situation and staging trials in advance of a formal or informal presentation ensures that fundamental mistakes can be avoided. It is not possible to know everything, or anticipate how something might be received, but careful preparation provides a useful and beneficial insight into the otherwise unknown.

The rehearsal of a presentation is not simply about physical communication and expression, but also about all the peripheral elements that complement the performance. Everything that can contribute to a message should be considered in advance as any minor miscalculation can have a dramatic impact.

Experiments with different methodologies and styles enable ideas to be evaluated and tailored to a particular audience. In addition to conveying a message it is important to listen and absorb responses.

Presentation

Practice breeds confidence and it is necessary to ensure that a presentation is interesting, accurate and concise. It is often more difficult to prepare a presentation that is short and direct than it would be to stage a longer experience. Some presentations are not formal occasions but rather more spontaneous affairs; these are situations where an opportunity is presented and a message needs to be communicated without any irrelevant distraction.

When thinking about the key elements of a presentation it can be helpful to ask whether the fundamental message could be communicated in an elevator, a corridor or during the journey on an escalator. Practising to get across a primary message in a restricted time span with limited resources, such as the time it takes to ride an escalator, ensures that information is focused and does not deviate.

If the basic story takes longer it is possible that an audience may become despondent and uninterested.

Practising a mantra or mental role play can allow a performance to be assimilated before it is transferred to others. In a situation where more time is afforded, and there is a captive audience, it is still necessary to ensure that the point or context is accessible from the outset. A scenario where props and additional supporting resources are available allows for interactivity and assists in maintaining the interest of the spectators. An agenda should be identified although it should not be rigorously adhered to if it is to the detriment of progress or a natural anecdote.

Short and sweet
Practise communicating all the essential elements of a presentation during a journey on an escalator to ensure that it is short and sweet – removing any excess issues.

Photography
Tim Harrison

Rehearsal *n.* a trial performance or practise of a play

'Few things – except, perhaps, Apple computer products and Moleskine notebooks – have been embraced by designers of all stripes so quickly and universally as Pecha Kucha Night has.'

20 Presenters, 20 Slides, 20 Seconds. Architect Magazine, US

Pecha Kucha Night

In 2003, the internationally acclaimed designers Astrid Klein and Mark Dytham created Pecha Kucha Night™, an event that brings young creatives together to share experiences, relay stories and network. Pecha Kucha is the Japanese sound for conversation, and Pecha Kucha Night provides the ideal opportunity for lively, engaging and informative presentations by keeping 'performances' to 20 slides, with each slide being allocated 20 seconds. A total presentation time of six minutes and 40 seconds ensures that the presenter stays focused and the audience remains attentive.

Pecha Kucha Nights around the world
Designers Astrid Klein and Mark Dytham established Klein Dytham Architecture in 1991 after working with the Tokyo-based designer Toyo Ito.

The international design awareness of KDa has seen the influential pair successfully engage design thinking in an array of disciplines and cultures and subsequently form the innovative and captivating Pecha Kucha Night in 2003. The incredible success of the event has seen it evolve in over 100 countries.

Statistics

Statistics should not be presented in a fashion that is tedious and uninspiring since they often represent stimulating and thought-provoking journeys. Information that is presented as facts and figures Is often the culmination of a broad range of exciting primary and secondary research processes all of which will have almost certainly involved meeting others and different cultural experiences.

Stimulate

If statistical information is presented in an apathetic format the potential and enthusiasm that was encountered prior to presentation can be drained away and lost. The research encounters and the positives that were experienced during the collection of information needs to be communicated in a mannor that allows the uninitiated to instantly understand, enjoy and retain. The information should stimulate not diminish interest.

The findings presented through statistics might be regarded as a springboard for the creative process and it is imperative that such information can inspire others. In a creative arena the concept of statistics is perhaps not as appealing as other activities. However, the information is vital and the research needs to be conducted. It is necessary that the production of information aligns with other modes of thinking and can engage and connect with the observer rather than isolate them.

Visual strategies

It is perhaps necessary to question what is needed by statistics. Is it simply reassurance, something that is able to confirm or refute a hypothesis? Or is it a process that is able to nudge and direct thinking along a certain pathway?

In situations where there is information overload or visual noise, it is possible for significant findings to be drowned by peripheral irrelevances. The language that is used to impart information should be accessible without obstruction.

The method employed to communicate the findings and the detail that they are presented in almost certainly depends on the type of project that is being considered and the stage that the information relates to in the design process.

Presentation of findings from initial enquiries often aims to set the scene and provide an indication of thinking. In such circumstances imagery and colour are often combined with simple phrases or figures to convey a particular point. The use of different visual strategies is engaging at different levels and assists in the connection, digestion and retention of information.

The reading of statistics is similar to the interpretation of an object, as it is the colour and the form that is initially appraised, followed by more abstract and theoretical information. If statistics are presented as a complicated mesh of figures it can be difficult for an outsider to find a starting point. The adoption of communicative, simple and relevant forms in conjunction with considered colour often provides a suitable trigger for initial comprehension.

Overview
A rethink and questioning of how conventional statistics are communicated enables alternative and more user-friendly methods to be explored. It is not always necessary to know the specific outcomes of research and occasionally, it is simply sufficient to have a general overview. A combination of colour, imagery and terminology supports the retention of information without being unduly complicated.

Design
Naomi Cheikh and Kevin Jackson

laptop   desktop

Effectiveness

In an attempt to communicate statistical information it is often necessary to make connections and appreciate what approaches are capable of stimulating interest – and those that might not be engaging. Previous, unfavourable experiences with charts and tables may subconsciously impair information if an alternative strategy is not encountered, something that is distinguishable and can demand attention.

Embracing or manipulating an appropriate image to function effectively within a presentation attracts interest and can subconsciously reaffirm a particular message.

Gantt charts, histograms and pie charts are perhaps amongst the most recognised vehicles for the communication of information, but care needs to be taken to ensure that findings are not seen as being turgid and uninspiring when presented in a mundane framework. Using the basic premise of familiar charts, information can be made considerably more visually stimulating through some aesthetic judgement and creative awareness. Why do segments need to be contained within a framework and why do they seldom show any relationship to the subject matter? Why do histograms remain bland towers, when the individual structures could be represented by something more akin to the subject matter being discussed?

Explore different professional and innovative methods of communicating information effectively without unnecessary embellishment. Every aspect incorporated within the message must make a contribution.

Computer usage statistics
Information on where students prefer to use their computer around the home (either bedroom, living room or office) is clearly communicated using simple imagery and colour.

Design
Naomi Cheikh and Kevin Jackson

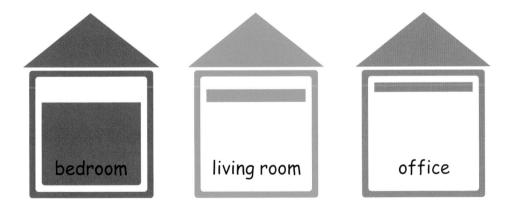

A designer who is passionate about what they do and enthusiastic about experimenting with ideas will not describe their work as 'this is just...' in a presentation. Instead it is imperative to get the story in a presentation right and this is achieved by conducting all the necessary groundwork.

Designer John O'Leary adopts a positive and imaginative role-play approach in the items he creates. Physical items are envisioned in a range of different and unfamiliar contexts and the rehearsal of different configurations or scenarios allows different stories and styles to be considered and evaluated. O'Leary studied Industrial Design at the National College of Art and Design in Dublin, Ireland and Furniture and Product Design at Edinburgh College of Art.

In 2004, he was awarded the Institute of Designers in Ireland Graduate Designer of the Year and was acknowledged as 'an excellent emerging design talent'. John O'Leary's ability to connect with design thinking and combine imagination with practicality is reflected within the beautiful items he has created.

The creative piece Congregate Communal Seating is an unusual and intriguing design, what was the design thinking behind the project?

Approaching the work with no preconceived ideas of what I wanted to produce, I let the history of the materials guide the project. This liberated the design process and, I feel, ultimately accounts for a more unique, interesting solution.

What were the materials that were used in the design and did their selection aim to portray a particular message?

I wanted to work with a material that had an interesting previous use with some worthwhile story to tell. I came across 100-year-old pitch pine pews that had been reclaimed from a local church.

Church pews as we know them were introduced during the Reformation in the fourteenth century to shape a more formal sermon with the pulpit as the focal point of church architecture and worship.

The final solution is an informal seating area that encourages multiple user interaction; in a sense, reincarnating the material full circle to its original roots. The piece has since been donated back to the church, which is now used as a community centre.

Congregate Communal Seating
An informal seating area that encourages multiple user interaction, made from 100-year-old pitch pine church pews.

Design
John O'Leary

Photography
John K. McGregor

The Apprentice Lamp appears to reflect a variety of messages. What was the inspiration for this work and does it fulfil the original objective?

Made by trainees learning the traditional craft of wood turning, the Apprentice Lamp is built from an assortment of turned sections made from reclaimed wood. The complexity of each section is dependent on the experience and ability of the trainee, increasing in difficulty as their skills improve. With no two sections identical, an infinite variety of lamps are possible.

I think this work does fulfil the original objective. By demonstrating the development and improvement of trainees' abilities as they progress from complete beginners to accomplished turners, the Apprentice Lamp supports a sense of achievement and enjoyment in learning new skills.

Training placements help to combat social exclusion, improve self-esteem, confidence and team working – contributing towards the individual's development and enhancing employability.

There appears to be an inherently natural approach to much of the design work that you create, what are your influences and why are they important?

Often the most interesting and rewarding work emerges from spontaneity and intuition. I am inspired by the work of the likes of Piet Hein Eek, Stuart Walker, Martino Gamper and Maarten Baas, all of whom work in an organic way that allows for experimentation and imperfection.

Their products are endearing, desirable and connect with the user on an emotional level that goes beyond purely the rational and functional.

Apprentice Lamp
Built from an assortment of turned section of reclaimed wood, with no two sections identical, an infinite variety of lamps is possible.

Design
John O'Leary

Photography
Stephen Kavanagh

Statistics > An interview with John O'Leary

The Vagabond Cabinet is a beautifully produced piece of design, which is wonderfully adorned with an eclectic array of abandoned handles. Is the story behind each handle fundamental to the design and are there any in particular which are unusual?

Certainly the door handles are what draws people to this piece. They seem to suggest intrigue, curiosity and wonder. They also add a playful element to the work, being described as 'eccentric' and 'Alice-in-Wonderland inspired'.

I spent the best part of a year collecting door handles, it became a bit of a strange obsession for me! I still have hundreds hoarded away, which I plan to use for future editions of the Vagabond range. Individually they are of little worth, however when viewed collectively I hope the user would begin to notice and appreciate the inherent beauty in everyday, mundane objects. This can help in alleviating some wasteful practices.

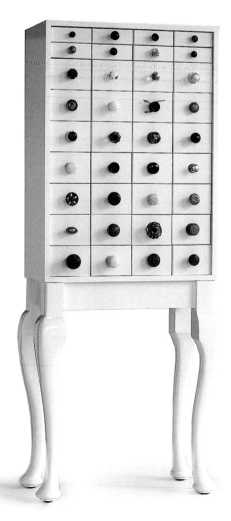

Performing

What was the reasoning behind the overall aesthetic of the Vagabond Cabinet?

Inspiration was originally drawn from the Wunderkrammer, or 'cabinet of wonders' and, in particular, cabinets of curiosities from Germany and the Netherlands produced in the seventeenth century. Inside, each drawer is unique, hand-crafted from different reclaimed woods, including brown oak, sycamore, walnut, birch plywood, chipboard and pine. Vagabond is an attempt to give value back to these materials, which were once disregarded as worthless junk.

Vagabond Cabinet of Curiosities
The high-gloss lacquer exterior and the tactile quality of the door knobs draw the user in and encourage them to interact with and look inside each drawer.

Design
John O'Leary

Photography
Stephen Kavanagh

During the initial stages of a design how do you like to record an idea?

I tend to carry a sketchbook with me wherever I go. That way I can note any thoughts or ideas or collect things of interest that I can easily refer to at a later date. Rough sketches and digital photographs are ideal for recording ideas quickly.

Mixed media is often utilised to communicate messages that cannot be captured through more conventional means. Do you use mixed media within your idea generation and how has it been incorporated?

Scrapbooks are a great way to collect and store mixed media, whether it is clippings from magazines or newspapers, photographs, sketches, interesting products, textures, colours, or anything of interest that may inspire further idea generation or exploration.

Conversing in a manner that is familiar or comfortable is not always the most appropriate method to employ. It is necessary to demonstrate empathy, understand what really needs to be said and appreciate how objects can be composed.

Alternative visual languages and dialogues need to be embraced to connect effectively and to ensure that a message is delivered in a relevant context. The pursuit of a suitable message requires experimentation and investigation, the need to test options and to challenge constraints.

The following projects have been compiled to encourage discovery and tempt enquiry. The unfamiliar can be disconcerting or uncomfortable; however, to veer from convention and move outside of a comfort zone it is necessary to embrace challenges, engage in the unknown and evaluate the outcome.

Model of mega-passenger aircraft
The incredible imagination of Luigi Colani and his advanced understanding of aesthetic language are demonstrated in the remarkable proposal for a mega-passenger aircraft. The visionary design was actually created in 1977 and took reference from the prehistoric, and extremely large, megalodon shark.

Design
Luigi Colani

Project 1
Inside out

The outer surface of a product is often
regarded as a protective façade, a face
that ensures that the delicate inner qualities
are cosseted and secure. Architecture and
fashion frequently demonstrate these qualities;
however, some products exhibit a shallow
exterior, which is undoubtedly beautiful and
attractive but only manages to shroud
something that might be considered as being
of a secondary nature. In situations where
the product might protect or store personal
belongings it is perhaps ironic that the lesser
qualities of the product, those under a refined
façade, are often those that are actually
in direct contact with the treasured items.
The surface of a bureau or a dresser often
flaunts the virtues of the creator and manages
to demonstrate emotional functionality, but
closer inspection can reveal an inner sanctum
that does not reflect such qualities.

Reversing the language of an object can
provide fascinating options and pathways.

Design a dresser that confronts expectation.
The external skin should be designed using
mass produced board or similar,
something that is strong and protective,
whilst the inner structure should embrace
a more distinguished approach.

The external appearance does not need to
be jeopardised due to the constraint imposed,
as the construction might use accepted and
customary approaches, and perhaps make
a feature out of any detrimental marks.

Project 2
Identical twins

Design constraints are often self-inflicted
or imposed due to a desire to either embark
on a creative challenge or because of
a fundamental necessity. A deliberate limit
on what can and cannot be pursued ensures
that familiar practices have to be modified
and adjusted, which inevitably opens up
innovative directions. A constraint does not
mean limited creativity, but rather expanded
vision and ingenuity.

Design and fabricate a school desk from
a suitable material and then recreate
the proposal using an alternative material.
The completed desks should aim to be
identical in appearance and must have
an identical weight. As the desks will have
different properties, it will be necessary
to search for options where mass can be
reduced or added to ensure that the proposals
are the same without any significant detriment
to the overall aesthetic.

Project 3
Old is new

When a product gets damaged it is often
considered to be unacceptable and
inadequate. In some circumstances a minor
impairment can mean an item is redundant
and is unfortunately cast aside. The language
a product projects undoubtedly changes
when its overall image is altered, marred
or revised, but there are also many occasions
when an item is deliberately blemished to
amend an intended message.

Identify products that have been intentionally
spoilt (enhanced) in order to modify
the original aesthetic language and consider
replicating the various dialogues into a
contemporary product.

Project 4
Knife and fork?

Stories are undeniably communicated
by silver and plastic cutlery, although it is
probable that the enhanced associations
attached to silver can be transposed
to plastic.

Is it the elegance, the decoration, or the
weight that is appealing with a silver knife and
fork, or is it simply that a plastic combination
feels cheap and has an inability to perform?

If a plastic set was beautifully decorated
in a style more akin to a sophisticated
silver set would it be an improvement or
simply kitsch? If the plastic set was as
balanced as the silver cutlery and associated
with a memorable occasion, would it remain
substandard? Is the judgement made on
expenditure alone?

What if a set was designed, that appeared
like a traditional silver set but was all in plastic
except one item that could not, in any way,
be distinguished from the others in the set?

Would the users all experience the sensation
of using silver or would they all experience
a feeling of plastic? Most of the users would
undoubtedly be using plastic but may retain
the sensation of silver.

Design an imitation product that projects
the language of a superior product.

Project 5
Secret messages

A secret message can be unveiled
when something smothering it is suddenly
erased and allows the underlying narrative
to surface and take prominence.
The retrieved story provides a momentary
glimpse of a previous generation,
an impression that has remained dormant
while all surrounding contexts evolved.

The disclosed item is often perfectly conserved
and is a significant resource for understanding
former dialogues and backgrounds.

Consider the different scenarios where
a tale from a previous era may be discovered
or exposed.

Project 6
Pure speculation

A subtle change in expression can make a substantial difference to the meaning of something being communicated. Although the constriction, restriction or expansion of a feature amends a message being projected it is particularly evident in delicate and slight objects where make-up may already be somewhat compromised.

Spectacles can be particularly sensitive to adjustments in configuration, and any minor alterations to the arrangement can significantly adjust the appearance of the product and user alike.

Design three sets of spectacles for a single user and explore how minor amendments to the structure of the products can notably influence the way in which the arrangements are perceived. The spectacles should avoid adornment and distracting features, but concentrate on the purity of the frame.

Project 7
It's raining!

A simple activity is often conducted habitually without actually appreciating the individual tasks that are involved. It is common to simply accept a process without thinking or deconstructing it to recognise what is occurring.

Produce a series of simple illustrations that suitably demonstrate the process of putting up an umbrella. The approach should capture the element of simple fun without being detrimental to the overall message. It will be necessary to distinguish between primary and secondary information and to appreciate that much of the message will be understood through simple representation.

Project 8
Swimwear

Swimwear often demonstrates a language that is analogous to fashion and contour design rather than product design, but if the approach to swimwear adopted an alternative narrative an array of opportunities could be presented. Classifying swimwear as a product might conjure up proposals to accommodate accessories such as sunglasses or creams in explicit compartments. Implementing unfamiliar elements in the design would be possible if a different attitude was allowed to induce thinking.

Design a piece of swimwear that assumes a product approach rather than a fashion mentality.

Project 9
Quick chat

How many marks does it take to communicate a message?

A product possesses a substantial amount of information, physical and emotional, but it is unlikely that all the different aspects can be communicated within a single sketch.

A hierarchy of information undoubtedly exists and what the object is, and the message that needs to be communicated, will influence the order and overall approach to an effective outline. The ability to punctuate a sketch and not include superfluous information ensures that a constructive representation can be accessed.

In a situation where an impression of an object needs to be captured efficiently, affording too much time to the process can be detrimental. Instinctive and intuitive expression is frequently more beneficial than an extended process.

Produce a series of sketches of a single product, over a monitored period, and aim to secure a faithful representation of the object. Reduce the amount of exposure to the object and evaluate the outcomes.

Repeat the process using an alternative medium.

Project 10
Role play

Role play is the process of acting out, pretending or engaging in an activity that is a simplified form of something more complicated. Role-play products are frequently produced for children to engage with so that they can emulate the activities that surround them or those that they might aspire to. A train driver, a spaceman, a nurse or a shopkeeper are all viable options for the child engaged in role play. The role-play product is a simplified version, a product that requires imagination and allows the user to ponder about certain possibilities. Role play is without complication and is a process to be enjoyed.

A playful language should not be solely restricted to products aimed at a younger generation as the processes that are followed form a valuable blueprint for objects for all ages.

Design a camera from a platform of play. The object should be simple and engaging to use, but should avoid the stereotypical outputs that are usually attached to products for children.

Project 11
White things

White has untold associations, such as being virginal, sterile, cold and pure – features that can be literally or laterally transposed onto objects in order to adopt the language. Consider the different descriptors that can be exploited to describe white and reflect on why these terms are appropriate. Following the investigation of white, design a black light that demonstrates the qualities of white. The light should aim for a creative translation of white rather than an actual representation. For example, a cold material may have a relationship to white but might not be white.

Project 12
Mind it

Generate a mind map based on the phrase 'storage' and subsequently design a product that encapsulates some of the elements that have been identified. A mind map is an important tool in discovering ideas, thoughts and feelings. It is an incredibly simple, but effective process that is endorsed and utilised by many leading designers. The approach is instinctive, creative and exciting and can be followed by children and adults alike.

A mind map allows for connections and links to be discovered and distant memories to be recalled, issues that might otherwise be overlooked or forgotten.

A single phrase, image or other relevant prompt is the initial focus of the map, which encourages subsequent thoughts to evolve. Embracing different triggers such as images, colour and words enables the individual to engage literal and lateral thinking strategies.

Select an image for the word 'story' and consider all the different ways, methods and associations to the term and allow ideas to flow from the centre.

The leading authority on Mind Maps is Tony Buzan www.buzanworld.com

Project 13
Love it, hate it

Inanimate objects undeniably reflect certain animate traits in a direct or indirect fashion. The terminology that is often used to describe a particular expression or attribute of an individual can be seen within the make-up of objects.

Using the following descriptors, conduct primary research to record the faces of individuals that demonstrate the identified characteristics. Continuing the investigation, locate products that further express these qualities in a holistic fashion: sad; smug; surprised; hostile; bashful; calm; shocked; belligerent; friendly; hopeful.

Evaluate the outcomes and consider how and why the images and objects recorded manage to make a particular connection.

Project 14
Being different

The medium selected for the delivery of a message undoubtedly influences the manner in which it is received and subsequently contextualised. Experimentation with unfamiliar media and mixed media can discover appropriate outcomes that are innovative and potentially more suitable than those that remain in the safe zone.

Depict, through the use of unfamiliar and varied media, a range of different emotions. Altering the venues for the production of the images and adjusting the scale of the outputs should be considered.

Project 15
Two per cent

If an image is reproduced and then further duplicates are produced from successive facsimiles, the work will eventually become so distorted that it may be difficult to appreciate that it was ever a descendant of the original. In extreme situations the quality can become so severely compromised due to the continual degradation that it might not even be recognised.

A similar process can be followed with a physical object where a subtle evolution of a form modifies the story that it is able to impart.

Select an object and systematically aim to remove two per cent of the outer façade in incremental stages in a subtle and controlled approach. The subtraction may be conducted by the elimination of a single component, the shaving of a surface or the deletion of a range of smaller features. The alteration of the object should not be particularly evident between direct stages, although it will undoubtedly be noticed between more significant junctures. As the stages are conducted, document the outcomes and compare the changing stories.

In contrast, select a similar object and aim to add two per cent to the outer skin in a systematic and uniformed approach. Again the addition should not be evident and only recognisable between significant increments. A thoughtful and careful approach should be employed to ensure that the approach or execution is not obvious.

Compare the contrast between the slightest and the more substantial outcomes.

Project 16
Shady look

An object can overshadow a smaller one when it is placed directly above it. The lesser, insignificant item can appear almost lost as it recedes into the shade, creating an impression that the overall space occupied by the two items is actually smaller. The controlled manipulation of objects allows for favourable, but inaccurate, statements to be made.

Selecting seven differently sized books, aim to configure the items so that the overall impact appears to be less than the entire collection at the outset. As the approach is modular, look to record and subsequently improve on the original findings. Adjusting the characteristics of the books selected may influence the intended deception.

Project 17
Sibling rivalry

The message that an object presents is influenced by the scale of the item, although the make-up of the object may itself be influenced by similar or analogous products of a contrasting dimension.

Thinking of a product in a different context but performing a parallel function enables languages to merge and unite.

The language of a flashlight is related to a headlight, which is akin to a chandelier or streetlight and ultimately, a floodlight. Although the scale and specific function evolves, the underlying language shares a common thread:

Flashlight > Headlight > Chandelier > Streetlight > Floodlight

Identify a product line that is separated through scale but where the individual items are fundamentally assigned a similar duty.

Produce a series of theme boards that recognise such sibling products and their universal language.

Project 18
Easy listening

A radio is often adorned with a whole range of seemingly insignificant and mundane information that clutter and mar its presentation. The visual balance of such objects is often adversely affected by trivial detail. Inane information that could undoubtedly be understood with a modicum of enquiry at the outset is often capable of tarnishing the long-term appearance and enjoyment of the object.

It is not uncommon for a radio or associated products to remain in their initial set-up stage; with subsequent adjustments to settings being rare as a single listener has preferences which are unlikely to change.

Design a radio that has an intuitive language and does not rely on symbols or legends to direct the user. The visual language of the radio should encourage interaction and recognise the importance of pre-requisite knowledge acquired from contact with analogous and comparable products.

Project 19
Makeover

A makeover refers to a change in appearance, an adjustment or series of alterations where something is purposefully enhanced, amended or exploited. It is an opportunity to consider things differently, make a statement and move on. A makeover does not need to be a radical investment that addresses all aspects and relationships associated with an object, but rather something that looks to instil life and vigour, something that generates a feel-good factor. A simple alteration can enable something to be seen in a more favourable or alternative light.

Seemingly trivial changes can substantially alter the visual language of an object and a reconfiguration of existing components without any actual changes to individual parts can make a vast difference to the original message.

Identify a collection of similar products or a family of items and deconstruct them to create a variety of components that are almost compatible. Using the knowledge acquired during their disassembly, rebuild the items and aim to interchange the components from the original objects. Although the items were initially considered to have a comparable relationship the subsequent exchange of parts creates hybrids with a completely different narrative. Continue to switch and substitute parts between the original items and appraise the different languages that are created.

Project 20
Luminosity dancing

There are many diverse styles of dance and an abundance of different artistic interpretations. Ballet, foxtrot, salsa, tap, rumba and disco are just a few of the various ways that dance can be performed, each having their own individual characteristics, twists and associations. Deconstructing dance and examining individual movements and meanings provides substantial material for the proposal of a delicate or graceful product, something that can capture and reflect the dancers' ability to delight.

There are many products that share the characteristics of dance and could evolve through studying the discipline. The associations with purity, elegance, sophistication, strength and beauty are perhaps particularly relevant to lighting, and referencing dance in the development of a light may mean that consideration is given to such qualities. An appreciation of dramatic effect and an ability to capture the essence of movement and shadow are also attributes that are often closely associated with both areas.

Design a light that has an identified characteristic of dance although it does not need to be an obvious relationship. Control over the story should be retained to ensure that an outcome does not digress unnecessarily. A literal translation of dance in the development of a light would probably mean that there would be no scope to manoeuvre the imagination, something that an abstract pathway may provide.

In an attempt to understand dance it is probable that it will be necessary to engage in primary research that may involve active participation or carefully observing a particular routine. It is unlikely that empathy with dance and the emergence of an appropriate lighting solution can be acquired through imagination and secondary referencing alone.

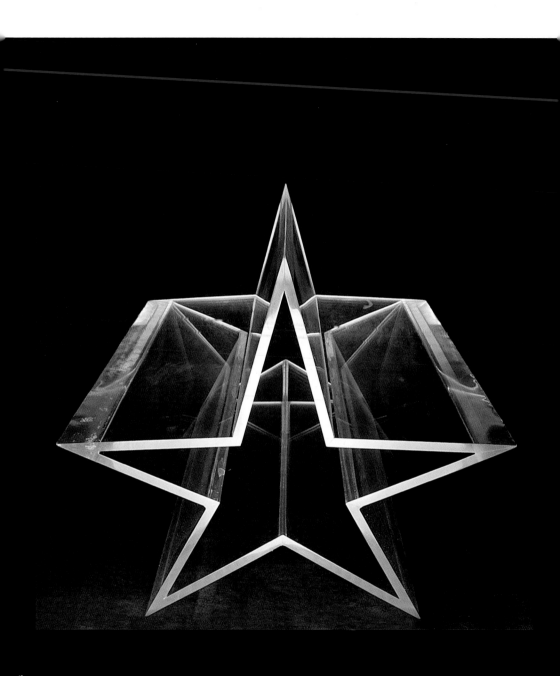

Visual conversations surround us and are a part of everyday life. Images and objects are constantly chattering, vying for individual attention, and although much might be missed or misunderstood a substantial amount is acknowledged through direct or subconscious means.

An awareness of visual languages develops as individual experiences expand, allowing bridges and connections to be fashioned that assist in the further understanding of more abstract and implied meanings. Everything has a story or a secret to divulge; the ability to recognise the subtle language indicators and triggers of images and objects stimulates intrigue and curiosity.

Starstruck acrylic seat
Starstruck, which was presented in Paris 2009, continues an imaginative collection of designs created by Pianeta Sud Est, where simple visual languages embrace a functional beauty.

Design
Valentina Audrito

A message does not need to be a labour of love, an intense and literal expression of something, but rather a simple representation that understands primary functions, one that is able to communicate the identified attributes effectively. It is usually the case that an experienced or confident designer can convey a convincing story with a minimum amount of physical effort.

The situation is similar to a conventional narrator who understands the significance and dramatic effect that a pause can create, and how it is a contrast to any dynamic content. It is often difficult to emulate the fluidity and natural ability of a master communicator, someone who has spent a lifetime understanding and practising the intricacies of the craft, as it is the unseen knowledge and experiential resources of an experienced individual that intuitively directs the message.

Accomplished artists are perhaps better known for their experimental, theoretical or abstract works, which frequently appear in the later stages of their studies rather than any prior technical investigations, which often form the foundation of their future knowledge and comprehension.

It is undoubtedly difficult to capture the essence or soul of an object without sustained practice and an intuitive understanding of function, but undeniably, instruction and exposure stimulate awareness. Images and objects can also be misread or misconstrued if they are placed out of context or if a third party is unaware of an underlying meaning. It is not necessarily a dire situation if something is misinterpreted and can occasionally lead to some original thinking and dialogues, but obviously the intention is to compose a message so that it can be easily understood.

The absent mind manages to inadvertently translate meanings and project alternative messages. The messages that are communicated through thoughtless acts are precious pointers to potential directions and opportunities.

A product can be composed to appeal to a particular individual and alienate others through the manipulation of form and structure. The ability to craft the message is similar to the way that a story is written to appeal to certain audiences, where certain traits and characteristics are employed to capture attention. The messages that a product communicates can be deceptive and intentionally misleading, or capable of distracting and it is not always the case that what is seen should be believed.

Objects and images tell stories, stories that must be carefully considered.

Glossary

Abstract
To take something away. An artwork that is abstracted has a particular feature or element removed.

Aesthetic
Fundamental principles connected to emotional perceptions and understanding of beauty, judgement and awareness.

Animate
To have life. An animate object has, in part, a characteristic of life.

Anthropologist
Anthropologists have an important role within the design process as they observe behaviour, mannerisms, attitudes and other attributes of individuals, societies and cultures, providing key information to consider.

Atypical
Something that is not expected or deviates from normal or typical practice or process.

Avant-garde
Refers to something that is considered to be unusual and experimental. A product that is thought to be avant-garde instigates, or inspires, an original direction or way of thinking.

Comfort zone
The comfort zone is effectively a state of mind that prevents individuals from experiencing the unknown. Such individuals tend to be less anxious in familiar surroundings. Exploring beyond a comfort zone may be to engage in a risk, but it is necessary to discover and gain original experiences.

Devil's advocate
The term 'devil's advocate' refers to an individual who poses a question, or expresses an unpopular opinion, to test the validity of something using different scenarios.

Disegno
Italian meaning 'drawing'.

Eclectic
A broad range of styles, ideas or similar, which can be brought together to inform direction and understanding.

Ephemeral
Something that has a limited life span or is used for a short amount of time.

Facsimile
An identical copy of something.

Genre
Refers to a certain style or classification of something.

Hackneyed
Something that has been utilised too often, is not original and does not excite.

Heterogeneous
Something that has a varied or assorted character.

Impressionistic
A subjective approach that is centred on feelings or opinions rather than an actual portrayal of something.

Inanimate
An object that is not alive or doesn't portray any evidence of living.

Inherent
Something that is an integral attribute from within or part of the make-up.

Innocuous
Something that is not offensive or harmful.

Innovate
To generate an original idea, method or market that has not been previously evident, in contrast to a reconfiguration that does not break boundaries.

Installation
An installation refers to a dedicated work of art that is set out or erected within an exhibition space.

Jargon
Language and terminology that is used inside specific disciplines, or cultures, that can be awkward for outsiders to comprehend. Jargon specific to different groups can have completely different meanings and further complicates understanding.

Juxtaposition
The placing or bringing together of different elements.

Lateral
Approaching or addressing something from the side or from a somewhat abstract perspective, rather than using the most obvious methods.

Literal
To contemplate or address something using the most obvious or fundamental form of approach is to take a literal view.

Mental baggage
Preconceived ideas of things, which prevent the development of original thought. Mental baggage can be a barrier to development, but can be overcome through the use of alternative approaches.

Mixed media
Mixed media refers to the use of different media in the creation of a single piece of artwork. There is no restriction to the media used and the process may include imagery and objects. The use of mixed media presents the opportunity to express particular messages that might not be possible using more conventional approaches.

Mnemonic
The development and understanding of how certain imagery, patterns and stories can be structured and utilised to assist the memory. There are many different mnemonic thoughts that individuals use to trigger memories.

Morphology
The structure or form of an object.

Narratives
The story that a product communicates through various means, including the statement associated with the configuration and composition, the emotive language and historical references.

Nomadic
Free to wander and having no permanent connections.

Nomenclature
The selection of names within a particular area.

Pecha kucha
Japanese meaning 'chit chat'.

Personification
The representation of a human attribute within a physical form

Primary research
Primary research is the gathering of research from first-hand experience and usually requires a 'go-out-and-do' approach. Types of primary research might include questionnaires, interviews or forums with a target audience. Approaches might also require the need to explore current markets and gain appreciation of current practices.

Secondary research
Secondary research can work in conjunction with primary research, but differs in the sense that it is the gathering of information that has already been published by a third party.

Semantics
Semantics refers to the particular meaning of a word or phrase in a specific context or scenario.

Semiology
The understanding of visual signs and symbols and their subsequent interpretation.

Shadowing
A process where the activity of another is better understood by joining them for a period of time to appreciate the situation first hand. Shadowing is a useful form of primary research that can provide detailed understanding. Shadowing provides a taste of what is occurring and possible directions to explore.

Shrouded
Refers to something that manages to envelop and hide, or obscure, something from being seen.

Somatic
Somatic means relating to the body rather than the mind.

Succinct
Something that is clear and concise as opposed to something that is expansive or lengthy.

Superfluous
Means unnecessary or something that is more than is needed.

Tangible
A physically existing item as opposed to an imaginary item or thought.

Tema e variazioni
Italian meaning 'variation of a theme' or 'variation of a topic'.

Piero Fornasetti (1913–1988) created the beautiful Tema e variazioni series having been moved by a striking photograph of the Italian opera singer Lina Cavalieri (1874–1944).

Touch-tronic
Touch-tronic objects are extremely sensitive and can be controlled with the slightest of contacts. The Lucellino table lamp designed by Ingo Maurer has a touch-tronic dimmer and on/off function that responds to the subtle touch of the brass wire supporting the bulb.

Trite
Something that has become too familiar and drab due to excessive exposure.

Trompe l'oeil
French meaning 'trick the eye'
or to 'fool the eye'.

Trompe l'oeil is a process where a
flat image is produced so that it appears
as a physical object with form.

Visceral
Connecting with profound emotions and
feeling rather than reason, judgement
or comprehension.

Zoomorphic
An object that is considered to have or reflect
animal forms, or gods in animal forms.

Glossary definitions in the chapters are taken
from the Concise Oxford English Dictionary.

Bibliography

Aldersey-Williams, H.
King and Miranda: The Poetry of the Machine
(Blueprint monographs) Fourth Estate (1991)

Antonelli, P.
**Humble Masterpieces:
100 Everyday Marvels of Design**
Thames & Hudson (2006)

Bakker, G. and Ramekers, R.
Droog Design – Spirit of the Nineties
010 Uitgeverij (1988)

Benyus, J.M.
Biomimicry
William Morrow (1997)

de Bono, E.
Six Thinking Hats
Penguin; 2nd revised edition (2000)

Börnsen-Holtmann, N.
Italian Design
Benedikt Taschen (1994)

Bramston, D.
Basics Product Design: Idea Searching
AVA Publishing (2008)

Bramston, D.
Basics Product Design: Material Thoughts
AVA Publishing (2009)

Buckminster Fuller, R.
Operating Manual for Spaceship Earth
Southern Illinois University Press (1969)

Buzan, T. and Buzan, B.
The Mind Map Book
BBC Active (2006)

Dempsey, A.
Styles, Schools and Movements
Thames & Hudson (2004)

De Noblet, J.
Industrial Design: Reflection of a Century
Flammarion (1993)

Dixon, P.
Futurewise: Six Faces of Global Change
Harper Collins (1998)

Dunne, A.
**Hertzian Tales: Electronic Products,
Aesthetic Experience, and Critical Design**
The MIT Press (2008)

Dunne, A. and Raby, F.
Design Noir: The Secret Life of Electronic Objects
August/Birkhauser (2001)

Fiell, C. and Fiell, P.
Design for the 21st Century
Taschen (2003)

Forty, A.
Objects of Desire
Thames & Hudson (1986)

Fuad-Luke, A.
The Eco-Design Handbook
Thames & Hudson (2002)

Fukasawa, N.
Naoto Fukasawa
Phaidon Press (2007)

Fulton Suri, J. and IDEO
Thoughtless Acts?
Chronicle Books (2005)

Gabra-Liddell, M.
Alessi: The Design Factory
Academy Editions (1994)

Gamper, M.
100 Chairs in 100 Days and its 100 Ways
Dent-De-Leone (2007)

Gershenfeld, N.
When Things Start to Think
Hodder & Stoughton (1999)

Hauffe, T.
Design: A Concise History
Laurence King Publishing (1998)

Kaku, M.
Visions
Oxford University Press (1998)

Kelley, T.
The Ten Faces of Innovation
Doubleday Business (2005)

Lupton, E.
Skin
Laurence King Publishing (2002)

MacCarthy, F.
British Design Since 1880
Lund Humphries (1982)

Meneguzzo, M.
Philippe Starck Distordre
Electra/Alessi (1996)

Moors, A.
Simply Droog
Droog Design, revised edition (2006)

Myerson, J.
IDEO: Masters of Innovation
Laurence King Publishing (2001)

Papanek, V.
The Green Imperative
Thames & Hudson (1995)

Philips Corporate Design
Vision of the Future
V+K Publishing (1996)

Pink, D.
A Whole New Mind
Cyan Books (2005)

Radice, B.
Ettore Sottsass: A Critical Biography
Thames & Hudson (1993)

Smith, P.
You Can Find Inspiration in Everything
Violette Editions (2001)

Sozzani, F.
Kartell
Skira Editore Milan (2003)

Sweet, F.
Frog: Form Follows Emotion
Thames & Hudson (1999)

Journals

Abitare
Artform
AZURE
Blueprint
b0x
Business Week
DEdiCate
Design
Design Week
domus
dwell
Egg
FRAME
frieze
FRUiTS
icon
I.D.
INNOVATION
Intramuros
Kult
Lowdown
made
MARK
Materials world
Metropolis magazine
mix
MODO
MONUMENT
newdesign
New Scientist
Product Design WORLD
Science magazine
Stuff
surface
T3
TWILL
vanidad
wallpaper
W magazine

Websites

www.basell.com
www.bayermaterialscience.com
www.cooperhewitt.org
www.core77.com
www.cosmit.it
www.csd.org
www.designboom.com
www.designmuseum.org
www.designspotter.com
www.dupont.com
www.geplastics.com
www.idsa.org
www.iom3.org
www.materialconnexion.com
www.moma.org
www.newdesigners.com
www.nhm.ac.uk
www.polymerlibrary.com
www.rsa.org.uk
www.sabic.com
www.sciencemuseum.com
www.tate.org.uk
www.TED.com
www.vam.ac.uk

Glossary > **Further resources** > Contacts

Contacts

www.alessi.com
www.amdl.it
www.antennadesign.com
www.avabooks.ch
www.biqquadro.com
www.buzanworld.com
www.canon.com
www.chrisjordan.com
www.clivemccarthy.com
www.colani.ch
www.colani.de
www.demakersvan.com
www.design.philips.com
www.disney.go.com
www.droog.com
www.dscience.com
www.dunneandraby.co.uk
www.eccoid.com
www.edwdebono.com
www.fabrica.it
www.fitch.com
www.fitnyc.edu
www.flos.com
www.fornasetti.com
www.francoaudritostudio65.com
www.fredrikfarg.com
www.frogdesign.com
www.frontdesign.se
www.gufram.com
www.hayonstudio.com
www.hudsonhotel.com
www.husseinchalayan.com
www.ideo.com
www.ilviogallo.it
www.industreal.it
www.ingo-maurer.com
www.isbg.co.uk
www.isseymiyake.com
www.jurgenbey.nl
www.kingmiranda.com
www.klein-dytham.com
www.lincoln.ac.uk
www.marc-newson.com
www.micheledelucchi.com
www.mikli.com
www.nike.com

www.ninetonine.es
www.oliver-schick.com
www.olivetti.com
www.pianeta-sudest.com
www.remyveenhuizen.nl
www.renault.com
www.rksdesign.com
www.siteenvirodesign.com
www.sony-europe.com
www.sottsass.it
www.starck.com
www.studiobramston.com
www.swatch.com
www.timothydonaldson.com
www.to22.net
www.tomvack.com
www.vibrazioniartdesign.com
www.yohjiyamamoto.co.jp

Visual conversations

Thank you to all the designers, artists and photographers who have supported the book and provided so many inspirational and visually stimulating images. Thank you also to the researchers and media-relation officers who have also assisted greatly in locating requested images and conducting searches in the relevant design archives.

The contribution of design sketches by Ettore Sottsass courtesy of Mrs Barbara Radice and Sottsass Associati, Michele De Lucchi, aMDL, Marc Newson, Marc Newson Ltd, Jaime Hayón, Hayon Studio, Ionna Vautrin & Guillaume Delvigne, Industreal, Todd Bracher, Efe Buluc and Mark Goetz, to22, Alessandro Mendini, Alessi, and Perry King & Santiago Miranda, King Miranda Design is really very much appreciated.

Visual Conversations aimed to include work from leading authorities on design, but also represent the creative outputs of young designers having an impact on design. The support and enthusiasm of the design community and the multinational companies that provided information is appreciated.

Many thanks also to the Lincoln School of Art & Design at the University of Lincoln, UK, and in particular the staff and students of the creative Product Design programme and the innovative Interactive Design programme.

Thank you to Malcolm Southward for the beautiful design of the book and ensuring that the images from all of the contributors have been sensitively and faithfully represented.

The selection of the front cover image was undoubtedly a difficult choice with so many creative images included within the book, however, the Fornasetti image captures the essence of the project and I am delighted that AVA Publishing selected it.

Finally, it is important to recognise and thank the incredible staff at AVA publishing and in particular my editor Georgia Kennedy who kept everything moving forward and to Helen Stone who managed to source many of the images from archives with her continual enquiry and liaison with various international designers, artists, photographers and researchers.

Thank you also to Caroline Walmsley and Brian Morris at AVA Publishing, who provided the opportunity to author the Visual Conversations title and provided the necessary support and drive for the book.

David Bramston 2009

Publisher's note

The subject of ethics is not new, yet its consideration within the applied visual arts is perhaps not as prevalent as it might be. Our aim here is to help a new generation of students, educators and practitioners find a methodology for structuring their thoughts and reflections in this vital area.

AVA Publishing hopes that these **Working with ethics** pages provide a platform for consideration and a flexible method for incorporating ethical concerns in the work of educators, students and professionals. Our approach consists of four parts:

The **introduction** is intended to be an accessible snapshot of the ethical landscape, both in terms of historical development and current dominant themes.

The **framework** positions ethical consideration into four areas and poses questions about the practical implications that might occur. Marking your response to each of these questions on the scale shown will allow your reactions to be further explored by comparison.

The **case study** sets out a real project and then poses some ethical questions for further consideration. This is a focus point for a debate rather than a critical analysis so there are no predetermined right or wrong answers.

A selection of **further reading** for you to consider areas of particular interest in more detail.

Ethical: aware-ness/ reflect-ion/ debate

Working with ethics

Introduction

Ethics is a complex subject that interlaces the idea of responsibilities to society with a wide range of considerations relevant to the character and happiness of the individual. It concerns virtues of compassion, loyalty and strength, but also of confidence, imagination, humour and optimism. As introduced in ancient Greek philosophy, the fundamental ethical question is *what should I do?* How we might pursue a 'good' life not only raises moral concerns about the effects of our actions on others, but also personal concerns about our own integrity.

In modern times the most important and controversial questions in ethics have been the moral ones. With growing populations and improvements in mobility and communications, it is not surprising that considerations about how to structure our lives together on the planet should come to the forefront. For visual artists and communicators it should be no surprise that these considerations will enter into the creative process.

Some ethical considerations are already enshrined in government laws and regulations or in professional codes of conduct. For example, plagiarism and breaches of confidentiality can be punishable offences. Legislation in various nations makes it unlawful to exclude people with disabilities from accessing information or spaces. The trade of ivory as a material has been banned in many countries. In these cases, a clear line has been drawn under what is unacceptable.

But most ethical matters remain open to debate, among experts and lay-people alike, and in the end we have to make our own choices on the basis of our own guiding principles or values. Is it more ethical to work for a charity than for a commercial company? Is it unethical to create something that others find ugly or offensive?

Specific questions such as these may lead to other questions that are more abstract. For example, is it only effects on humans (and what they care about) that are important, or might effects on the natural world require attention too?

Is promoting ethical consequences justified even when it requires ethical sacrifices along the way? Must there be a single unifying theory of ethics (such as the Utilitarian thesis that the right course of action is always the one that leads to the greatest happiness of the greatest number), or might there always be many different ethical values that pull a person in various directions?

As we enter into ethical debate and engage with these dilemmas on a personal and professional level, we may change our views or change our view of others. The real test though is whether, as we reflect on these matters, we change the way we act as well as the way we think. Socrates, the 'father' of philosophy, proposed that people will naturally do 'good' if they know what is right. But this point might only lead us to yet another question: *how do we know what is right?*

You
What are your ethical beliefs?

Central to everything you do will be your attitude to people and issues around you. For some people their ethics are an active part of the decisions they make everyday as a consumer, a voter or a working professional. Others may think about ethics very little and yet this does not automatically make them unethical. Personal beliefs, lifestyle, politics, nationality, religion, gender, class or education can all influence your ethical viewpoint.

Using the scale, where would you place yourself? What do you take into account to make your decision? Compare results with your friends or colleagues.

Your client
What are your terms?

Working relationships are central to whether ethics can be embedded into a project and your conduct on a day-to-day basis is a demonstration of your professional ethics. The decision with the biggest impact is whom you choose to work with in the first place. Cigarette companies or arms traders are often-cited examples when talking about where a line might be drawn, but rarely are real situations so extreme. At what point might you turn down a project on ethical grounds and how much does the reality of having to earn a living affect your ability to choose?

Using the scale, where would you place a project? How does this compare to your personal ethical level?

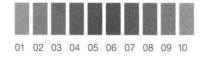

01 02 03 04 05 06 07 08 09 10

01 02 03 04 05 06 07 08 09 10

Your specifications
What are the impacts of your materials?

In relatively recent times we are learning that many natural materials are in short supply. At the same time we are increasingly aware that some man-made materials can have harmful, long-term effects on people or the planet. How much do you know about the materials that you use? Do you know where they come from, how far they travel and under what conditions they are obtained? When your creation is no longer needed, will it be easy and safe to recycle? Will it disappear without a trace? Are these considerations the responsibility of you or are they out of your hands?

Using the scale, mark how ethical your material choices are.

Your creation
What is the purpose of your work?

Between you, your colleagues and an agreed brief, what will your creation achieve? What purpose will it have in society and will it make a positive contribution? Should your work result in more than commercial success or industry awards? Might your creation help save lives, educate, protect or inspire? Form and function are two established aspects of judging a creation, but there is little consensus on the obligations of visual artists and communicators toward society, or the role they might have in solving social or environmental problems. If you want recognition for being the creator, how responsible are you for what you create and where might that responsibility end?

Using the scale, mark how ethical the purpose of your work is.

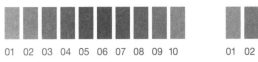

01 02 03 04 05 06 07 08 09 10   01 02 03 04 05 06 07 08 09 10

Working with ethics

One aspect of product design that raises an ethical dilemma is the environmental impact that materials can have. This issue needs more consideration, particularly if an object is knowingly designed to become waste after only a short time. The advent of synthetic plastics in the early 20th century opened the door to mass production of cheap, attractive goods that democratised the ownership of consumer products.

Planned obsolescence became a lucrative strategy for large companies in the 1950s and this fuelled ongoing product replacements through styling changes. But as the longer-term impacts of manmade plastics became more widely understood in the second half of the 20th century, it has become clear that there is an environmental price to pay for human convenience and consumer choice. How much responsibility should a product designer have in this situation? If designers wish to minimise the environmental impacts of products, what might they most usefully do?

Newspaper editor László Bíró (1899–1985), found that he wasted a lot of time cleaning up smudges and tearing pages with the nib of his fountain pen. With help from his brother, Bíró began to work on a new type of pen and fitted a tiny ball in its tip that was free to turn in a socket. He filed a British patent for the design in June 1938.

In 1945, Marcel Bich, along with his partner Edouard Buffard, bought a factory in France and went into business as the maker of parts for fountain pens and mechanical lead pencils. As his business began to grow, the development of the ballpoint pen was advancing in both Europe and the US. Bich saw the great potential for this new writing instrument and obtained the patent rights from Bíró to manufacture his own. In 1950, Bich launched his new reliable pen at an affordable price.

The BIC biro was a mass-produced consumer item that was cheap enough that if it were lost, the owner would be unlikely to care. Its mass success comes out of the BIC product philosophy: 'just what is necessary', a phrase driven by simplicity, functionality, quality and price. The aim is for harmony between the form of a product and the use it is designed for.

A BIC pen can draw a line up to three kilometers long. It is made from polystyrene (transparent barrel), polypropylene (cap), tungsten carbide (ball) and brass/nickel silver (tip). The environmental impact of a BIC biro comes predominantly from the materials, with approximately five grams of oil-based plastic used in the manufacture of each pen. Because of their widespread use by schoolchildren, all ballpoint ink formulas are non-toxic and the manufacturing and content of ink is regulated in most countries.

The relatively recent addition of the vent hole in the cap of the BIC pen was designed to minimise the risk of choking should it be swallowed. This is a requirement to comply with international safety standards after an incident in the late 1980s where a young child in the UK died due to the inhalation of a pen cap. Nine similar deaths had been recorded in the previous fifteen years, none have been recorded in the UK since the publication of this safety standard.

The BIC biro has become an industrial design classic. In 2002 it entered the permanent collections of the Museum of Modern Art (MOMA) in New York. In September 2005, BIC sold its one hundred billionth disposable ballpoint, making it the world's best-selling pen.

Should designers, producers or users have responsibility if a product causes injury?

Is it unethical to design a product to be thrown away?

Would you have worked on this project?

Our definitions of positive impact have become too narrow as designers. Focused perhaps too often on pleasing our own ego.

Tim Brown
(CEO of IDEO)
From a transcription of a presentation given at the *InterSections* conference in 2007

Working with ethics

Further reading

AIGA
Design Business and Ethics
2007, AIGA

Eaton, Marcia Muelder
Aesthetics and the Good Life
1989, Associated University Press

Ellison, David
Ethics and Aesthetics in European Modernist Literature:
From the Sublime to the Uncanny
2001, Cambridge University Press

Fenner, David E W (Ed)
Ethics and the Arts:
An Anthology
1995, Garland Reference Library of Social Science

Gini, Al and Marcoux, Alexei M
Case Studies in Business Ethics
2005, Prentice Hall

McDonough, William and Braungart, Michael
Cradle to Cradle:
Remaking the Way We Make Things
2002, North Point Press

Papanek, Victor
Design for the Real World:
Making to Measure
1972, Thames and Hudson

United Nations
Global Compact the Ten Principles
www.unglobalcompact.org/AboutTheGC/TheTenPrinciples/index.html